CIMA's CGMA® 2019 Professional Examinations

CIMA's CGMA Certificate in Business Accounting

AF875256

Subject BA3

Fundamentals of Financial Accounting

EXAM PRACTICE KIT

CIMA

KAPLAN PUBLISHING

British Library Cataloguing-in-Publication Data

A catalogue record for this book is available from the British Library.

ISBN: 978-1-83735-079-7

Printed and bound in Great Britain

Published by: Kaplan Publishing UK

Unit 2 The Business Centre, Molly Millars Lane, Wokingham, Berkshire. RG41 2QZ

Notice

The text in this material and any others made available by any Kaplan Group company does not amount to advice on a particular matter and should not be taken as such. No reliance should be placed on the content as the basis for any investment or other decision or in connection with any advice given to third parties. Please consult your appropriate professional adviser as necessary. Kaplan Publishing Limited, all other Kaplan group companies, the International Accounting Standards Board, and the IFRS Foundation expressly disclaim all liability to any person in respect of any losses or other claims, whether direct, indirect, incidental, consequential or otherwise arising in relation to the use of such materials. Printed and bound in Great Britain.

Kaplan is not responsible for the content of external websites. The inclusion of a link to a third party website in the text should be not taken as an endorsement.

Kaplan Publishing's learning materials are designed to help students succeed in their examinations. In certain circumstances, CIMA can make post-exam adjustment to a student's mark or grade to reflect adverse circumstances which may have disadvantaged a student's ability to take an exam or demonstrate their normal level of attainment (see CIMA's Special Consideration policy). However, it should be noted that students will not be eligible for special consideration by CIMA if preparation for or performance in a CIMA exam is affected by any failure by their tuition provider to prepare them properly for the exam for any reason including, but not limited to, staff shortages, building work or a lack of facilities etc.

Similarly, CIMA will not accept applications for special consideration on any of the following grounds:

- failure by a tuition provider to cover the whole syllabus
- failure by the student to cover the whole syllabus, for instance as a result of joining a course part way through
- failure by the student to prepare adequately for the exam, or to use the correct pre-seen material
- errors in the Kaplan Official Study Text, including sample (practice) questions or any other Kaplan content or
- errors in any other study materials (from any other tuition provider or publisher).

Acknowledgements

This product contains copyright material and trademarks of the IFRS Foundation®. All rights reserved. Used under licence from the IFRS Foundation®. Reproduction and use rights are strictly limited. For more information about the IFRS Foundation and rights to use its material please visit www.ifrs.org.

CONTENTS

Section

This document references IFRS® Standards and IAS® Standards, which are authored by the International Accounting Standards Board (the Board), and published in the 2024 IFRS Standards Red Book.

Quality and accuracy are of the utmost importance to us so if you spot an error in any of our products, please send an email to mykaplanreporting@kaplan.com with full details.

Our Quality Co-ordinator will work with our technical team to verify the error and take action to ensure it is corrected in future editions.

INDEX TO QUESTIONS AND ANSWERS

OBJECTIVE TEST QUESTIONS

SYLLABUS GUIDANCE, LEARNING OBJECTIVES AND VERBS

CIMA's CGMA® 2019 PROFESSIONAL QUALIFICATION

Details regarding the content of CIMA's CGMA 2019 Professional Qualification can be located within the CGMA 2019 Professional Qualification syllabus document.

You can use the following diagram showing the whole structure of your qualification to help you keep track of your progress. Make sure you seek appropriate advice if you are unsure about your progression through the qualification.

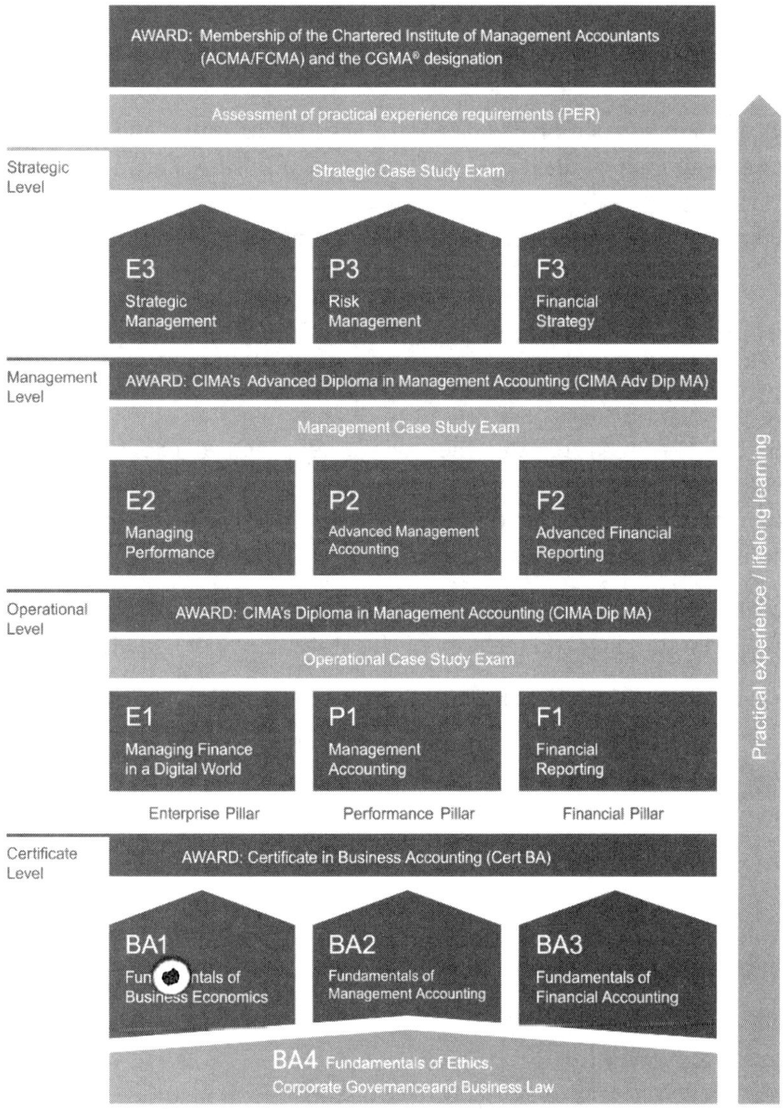

Reproduced with CIMA's permission

A THE CERTIFICATE IN BUSINESS ACCOUNTING (CERT BA)

The Cert BA provides a foundation in the essential elements of accounting and business. This includes the Fundamentals of Business Economics. There are four subject areas, which are all tested by computer-based assessment (CBA). The four subjects are:

- BA1: Fundamentals of Business Economics
- BA2: Fundamentals of Management Accounting
- BA3: Fundamentals of Financial Accounting
- BA4: Fundamentals of Ethics, Corporate Governance and Business Law

The Cert BA is both a qualification in its own right and an entry route to the next stage in CIMA's examination structure.

The examination structure after the Certificate comprises:

- Operational Level
- Managerial Level
- Strategic Level

The CIMA Qualification includes more advanced topics in Accounting and Business. It is therefore very important that you apply yourself to Fundamentals of Business Economics, not only because it is part of the Certificate, but also as a platform for more advanced studies. It is thus an important step in becoming a qualified member of the Chartered Institute of Management Accountants.

B AIMS OF THE SYLLABUS

The aims of the syllabus are

- to provide for the Institute, together with the practical experience requirements, an adequate basis for assuring society that those admitted to membership are competent to act as management accountants for entities, whether in manufacturing, commercial or service organisations, in the public or private sectors of the economy;
- to enable the Institute to examine whether prospective members have an adequate knowledge, understanding and mastery of the stated body of knowledge and skills;
- to complement the Institute's practical experience and skills development requirements.

C STUDY WEIGHTINGS

A percentage weighting is shown against each topic in the syllabus. This is intended as a guide to the proportion of study time each topic requires.

All topics in the syllabus must be studied, since any single examination question may examine more than one topic, or carry a higher proportion of marks than the percentage study time suggested.

The weightings do not specify the number of marks that will be allocated to topics in the examination.

D CIMA'S HIERARCHY OF LEARNING OBJECTIVES

CIMA places great importance on the definition of verbs in structuring Objective Test Examinations. It is therefore crucial that you understand the verbs in order to appreciate the depth and breadth of a topic and the level of skill required. The CIMA Cert BA syllabus learning outcomes and objective test questions will focus on levels one, two and three of the CIMA's hierarchy of learning objectives (knowledge, comprehension and application). However, as you progress to the Operational, Management and Strategic levels of the CIMA Professional Qualification, testing will include levels four and five of the hierarchy. As you complete your CIMA Professional Qualification, you can therefore expect to be tested on knowledge, comprehension, application, analysis and evaluation.

In CIMA Cert BA Objective Test Examinations you will meet verbs from only levels 1, 2, and 3 of the hierarchy which are as follows:

Skill level	Verbs used	Definition
Level 1 **Knowledge** What you are expected to know	List	Make a list of
	State	Express, fully or clearly, the details/facts of
	Define	Give the exact meaning of
	Outline	Give a summary of

For example you could be asked to define economic terms such as 'inflation' (BA1), or to define the term 'management accounting' (BA2) or to state the accounting entries required to record the revaluation surplus arising on revaluation of land and buildings (BA3).

Skill level	Verbs used	Definition
Level 2 **Comprehension** What you are expected to understand	Describe	Communicate the key features of
	Distinguish	Highlight the differences between
	Explain	Make clear or intelligible/state the meaning or purpose of
	Identify	Recognise, establish or select after consideration
	Illustrate	Use an example to describe or explain something

For example you could be asked to explain the components of the circular flow of funds (BA1), or distinguish between financial accounting and management accounting (BA3) or distinguish between express terms and implied terms of a contract of employment (BA4).

Skill level	Verbs used	Definition
Level 3 Application How you are expected to apply your knowledge	Apply	Put to practical use
	Calculate	Ascertain or reckon mathematically
	Conduct	Organise and carry out
	Demonstrate	Prove with certainty or exhibit by practical means
	Prepare	Make or get ready for use
	Reconcile	Make or prove consistent/compatible

For example you could be asked to reconcile the differences between profits calculated using absorption costing and marginal costing (BA2), or to calculate the gain or loss on disposal of a non-current asset (BA3) or to apply relevant principles to determine the outcome of a law-based or ethical problem (BA4).

For reference, levels 4 and 5 of the hierarchy require demonstration of analysis and evaluation skills respectively. Further detail on levels 4 and 5 of the hierarchy which are tested in the CIMA Professional Qualification can be obtained from the CIMA website, www.aicpa-cima.com.

OBJECTIVE TESTS

Objective Test questions require you to choose or provide a response to a question whose correct answer is predetermined.

The most common types of Objective Test question you will see are:

- **multiple choice**, where you have to choose the correct answer(s) from a list of possible answers – this could either be numbers or text.
- **multiple response** with more choices and answers, for example, choosing two correct answers from a list of five available answers – this could either be numbers or text.
- **number entry**, where you give your numeric answer to one or more parts of a question, for example, gross profit is $25,000 and the accrual for heat and light charges is $750.
- **drag and drop**, where you match one or more items with others from the list available, for example, matching several accounting terms with the appropriate definition
- **drop down**, where you choose the correct answer from those available in a drop down menu, for example, choosing the correct calculation of an accounting ratio, or stating whether an individual statement is true or false. This can also be included with a number entry style question.
- **hot spot**, where, for example, you use your computer cursor or mouse to identify the point of profit maximisation on a graph

CIMA has provided the following guidance relating to the format of questions and their marking:

- questions which require narrative responses to be typed will not be used
- for number entry questions, clear guidance will usually be given about the format in which the answer is required e.g. 'to the nearest $' or 'to two decimal places'.
- item set questions provide a scenario which then forms the basis of more than one question (usually 2 and 4 questions). These sets of questions would appear together in the test and are most likely to appear in BA2 and BA3
- all questions are independent so that, where questions are based on a common item set scenario, each question will be distinct and the answer to a later question will not be dependent upon answering an earlier question correctly
- all items are equally weighted and, where a question consists of more than one element, all elements must be answered correctly for the question to be marked correct.

Throughout this Exam Practice Kit we have introduced these types of questions, but obviously we have had to label answers A, B, C etc. rather than using click boxes. For convenience we have retained quite a few questions where an initial scenario leads to a number of sub-questions. There will be questions of this type in the Objective Test Examination but they will rarely have more than three sub-questions.

Guidance re CIMA on-screen calculator

As part of the CIMA Objective Test software, candidates are provided with a calculator. This calculator is on-screen and is available for the duration of the assessment. The calculator is available in Objective Test Examinations for BA1, BA2 and BA3 (it is not required for BA4).

Guidance regarding calculator use in the Objective Test Examinations is available online at: https://connect.cimaglobal.com/

CIMA Cert BA Objective Tests

The Objective Tests are a two-hour assessment comprising compulsory questions, each with one or more parts. There will be no choice and all questions should be attempted. The number of questions in each assessment are as follows:

BA1 Fundamentals of Business Economics – 60 questions

BA2 Fundamentals of Management Accounting – 60 questions

BA3 Fundamentals of Financial Accounting – 60 questions

BA4 Fundamentals of Ethics, Corporate Governance and Business Law – 85 questions

SYLLABUS OUTLINE

BA3: Fundamentals of Financial Accounting

Syllabus overview

The main objective of this subject is to obtain a practical understanding of financial accounting and the process behind the preparation of financial statements for single entities.

These statements are prepared within a conceptual and regulatory framework requiring an understanding of the role of legislation and of accounting standards. The need to understand and apply necessary controls for accounting systems, and the nature of errors is also covered. There is an introduction to measuring financial performance with the calculation of basic ratios.

Note: Students are required to be aware of the format and content of published accounts but are not required to prepare them. No detailed knowledge of any specific accounting treatment contained in the International Financial Reporting Standards (IFRSs) – including the International Accounting Standards (IASs) – is necessary, except in terms IAS 2 and the treatment of inventory, IAS 16 and IAS 38 for basic non-current asset transactions.

IAS 1 and IAS 7 formats will form the basis of the financial statements. The terminology used for all entities will be that of International Financial Reporting Standards. This will enable students to use a consistent set of accounting terms throughout their studies.

Assessment strategy

There will be a two hour computer based assessment, comprising 60 compulsory objective test questions. Short scenarios may be given to which one or more objective test questions relate.

Syllabus structure

The syllabus comprises the following topics and weightings:

Content area		Weighting
A	Accounting principles, concepts and regulations	10%
B	Recording accounting transactions	50%
C	Preparation of accounts for single entities	30%
D	Analysis of financial statements	10%
		100%

LEARNING OUTCOMES AND INDICATIVE SYLLABUS CONTENT

BA3A: Accounting principles, concepts and regulations (10%)

Learning outcomes

On completion of their studies, students should be able to:

Lead	Component	Level	Indicative syllabus content
1. Explain the principles and concepts of financial accounting.	a. Explain the need for accounting records. b. Identify the needs of different user groups. c. Distinguish between the purposes of financial and management accounts. d. Explain capital and revenue, cash and profit, income and expenditure, assets and liabilities. e. Explain the underlying assumptions, policies and accounting estimates. f. Identify the need for and information to be included in an integrated report. g. Describe the accounting equation. h. Explain the need for accounting codes.	2 2 2 2 2 2 2 2	• Accounting records to be kept and their uses; concept of stewardship. • Users of accounts and their information needs. • Functions of financial and management accounts; purpose of accounting statements. • Capital and revenue; cash and profit; income, expenditure, assets and liabilities. • Underlying assumptions, policies, accounting estimates; historical cost convention; qualitative characteristics of the Framework, elements of financial statements. • The principles and elements of the Framework for integrated reporting. • The accounting equation formula. • Use of coding in record keeping.
2. Explain the impact of the regulatory framework on financial accounting.	a. Explain the influence of legislation and accounting standards on published accounting information.	2	• Regulatory influence of company law; role of accounting standards; IASs and IFRSs; formats for published accounts.

BA3B: Recording accounting transactions (50%)

Learning outcomes

On completion of their studies, students should be able to:

Lead	Component	Level	Indicative syllabus content
1. Prepare accounting records.	a. Prepare the books of prime entry. b. Apply the principles of double- entry bookkeeping. c. Prepare nominal ledger accounts. d. Prepare the trial balance. e. Explain the nature of accounting errors. f. Prepare accounting entries for the correction of errors. g. Prepare accounting entries for non-current assets. h. Prepare a non-current asset register.	3 3 3 3 2 3 3 3	• Record sales, purchase, income and expense transactions in the sales day book, purchase day book, cash book, returns books, and sales/purchase ledger. • The accounting equation; double-entry bookkeeping rules; journal entries. • Record all types of business transactions in nominal ledger accounts. • Completing the trial balance from given ledger account balances. • Errors including those of principle, omission, and commission. • Journal entries and suspense accounts. • In accordance with IAS 16 – acquisition, depreciation (straight line, reducing balance), revaluation, impairment and disposal of tangibles. • In accordance with IAS 38 – intangibles and amortisation. • Information to be recorded in a non-current asset register.
2. Prepare accounting reconciliations.	a. Prepare bank reconciliation statements. b. Prepare petty cash statements under an imprest system. c. Prepare sales and purchase ledger control account reconciliations.	3 3 3	• Reconciliation of the cashbook to the bank statement. • Using the imprest system for petty cash. • Reconciliation of sales and purchase ledger control accounts to sales and purchase ledgers.
3. Prepare accounting entries for specific transactions.	a. Calculate sales tax. b. Prepare accounting entries for sales tax. c. Prepare accounting entries for payroll. d. Prepare accounting entries for the issue of shares.	3 3 3 3	• Calculation of sales tax on all business transactions. • Accounting entries for sales tax. **Note:** No knowledge of any specific tax systems/rules/rates will be required. • Accounting entries for basic payroll information. **Note:** No knowledge of any specific income tax rules will be required. • Issue at full market price, rights issue and bonus issue.

BA3C: Preparation of accounts for single entities (30%)

Learning outcomes

On completion of their studies, students should be able to:

Lead	Component	Level	Indicative syllabus content
1. Prepare accounting adjustments.	a. Prepare accounting entries for accruals and prepayments. b. Prepare accounting entries for irrecoverable debts and allowances for receivables. c. Prepare accounting entries for inventories.	3 3 3	• Calculations and journals for accruals and prepayments (income and expenses). • Prepare journals for irrecoverable debts and allowances for receivables from given information. • In accordance with IAS 2 – calculation of the figure for closing inventory for inclusion in the financial statements (FIFO, LIFO and average cost) and the journal entry to record it.
2. Prepare manufacturing accounts.	a. Prepare basic manufacturing accounts.	3	• Manufacturing accounts produced from given information. **Note:** No calculation of overheads and inventory balances is required.
3. Prepare financial statements for a single entity.	a. Prepare financial statements from a trial balance. b. Prepare financial statements from incomplete records. c. Prepare a statement of cash flows.	3 3 3	• In accordance with IAS 1 – Statement of profit or loss and other comprehensive income; statement of financial position; statement of changes in equity. • Calculate missing numbers using the accounting equation, profit margins and mark-ups, receivables and payables ledgers, and cash and bank ledgers. • In accordance with IAS 7 – operating, investing and financing sections.

BA3D: Analysis of financial statements (10%)

Learning outcomes

On completion of their studies, students should be able to:

Lead	Component	Level	Indicative syllabus content
1. Identify information provided by accounting ratios.	a. Identify the information provided by the calculation of accounting ratios. b. Identify reasons for the changes in accounting ratios.	2 2	• Information provided by accounting ratios. • Reasons for the changes in accounting ratios.
2. Calculate basic accounting ratios.	a. Calculation of profitability ratios. b. Calculation of liquidity ratios. c. Calculation of risk ratios.	3 3 3	• Ratios: return on capital employed; gross, operating and net profit margins; non-current asset turnover. • Trade receivables collection period and trade payables payment period; current and quick ratios; inventory turnover. • Gearing and interest cover.

Information concerning formulae and tables will be provided via the AICPA & CIMA website, www.aicpa-cima.com.

Section 1

OBJECTIVE TEST QUESTIONS

ACCOUNTING PRINCIPLES, CONCEPTS AND REGULATIONS

EXPLAIN THE PRINCIPLES AND CONCEPTS OF FINANCIAL ACCOUNTING

1 Which THREE of the following are accounting conventions?

A Prudence

B Consistency

C Depreciation

D Accruals

2 Capital maintenance is important for:

A the sources of finance

B the measurement of profit

C the relationship of debt to equity

D the purchase of non-current assets

3 If, at the end of the financial year, a an entity makes a charge against the profit for stationery consumed but not yet invoiced, this adjustment is in accordance with the convention of:

A materiality

B accruals

C consistency

D objectivity

4 Drag the correct wording from the following list to complete the sentence regarding the historical cost convention.

The historic cost convention ______________________.

- fails to take account of changing price levels over time
- records only past transactions
- values all assets at their cost to the business, without any adjustment for depreciation
- has been replaced in accounting records by a system of current cost accounting

5 Drag and drop the following options to complete the statement below.

In times of rising prices, the historical cost convention has the effect of _________ profits and ________ the statement of financial position asset values

Drag and drop options: overstating, understating (the options can be used more than once)

6 Sales revenue should be recognised only when goods and services have been supplied.

The accounting convention that governs the above is the:

A accruals convention

B materiality convention

C realisation convention

D dual aspect convention

7 The term capital maintenance implies that:

A the capital of a business should be kept intact by not paying our dividends

B a business should invest its profits in the purchase of capital assets

C non-current assets should be properly maintained

D profit is earned only if the value of an organisation's net assets or its operating capability has increased during the accounting period

8 The accounting convention that requires non-current assets to be valued at cost less accumulated depreciation, rather than their enforced saleable value, is the

A net realisable value convention

B prudence convention

C realisation convention

D going concern convention

9 Which THREE of the following are necessary elements of the stewardship function?

A To maximise profits

B To safeguard assets

C To ensure adequate controls exist to prevent or detect fraud

D To prepare the financial accounts

E To attend meetings with the bank

F To prepare management accounts

10 Which one of the following provides the most appropriate definition of bookkeeping?

A To calculate the amount of dividend to pay to shareholders

B To record, categorise and summarise financial transactions

C To provide useful information to users

D To calculate the taxation due to the government

11 Drag and drop the options below into the table provided to identify whether each of the items below would change the capital of a sole proprietor.

- A payable being paid the amount due by cheque
- Raw materials being purchased on credit
- Non-current assets being purchased on credit
- Wages being paid in cash

Change	No change

12 In accordance with the IASB® Conceptual Framework for Financial Reporting what is the main aim of financial reporting?

A To record every financial transaction individually

B To maintain ledger accounts for every transaction

C To prepare a trial balance

D To provide financial information to users of such information

13 The profit of a business may be calculated by using which one of the following formula?

A Opening capital – Drawings + Capital introduced – Closing capital

B Opening capital + Drawings – Capital introduced – Closing capital

C Closing capital + Drawings – Capital introduced – Opening capital

D Closing capital – Drawings + Capital introduced – Opening capital

14 Do the comments below relate to management or financial accounting? Drag each comment under the correct heading.

	Management accounting	Financial accounting
Uses historical data		
Is a legal requirement		
Uses both financial and non-financial information		
Is normally prepared annually		

15 Which THREE of the following are qualitative characteristics of financial statements as per the Conceptual Framework for Financial Reporting?

A Relevance

B Profitability

C Comparability

D Completeness

16 Select the correct wording to complete each of the following sentences relating to management accounting and financial accounting.

A Recording all transactions in the books of accounts is an aim of financial/ management accounting.

B Providing management with detailed analyses of costs is an aim of financial/ management accounting.

C Presenting the financial results of the organisation by means of recognised statements is an aim of financial/management accounting.

D Calculating profit is an aim of financial/management accounting.

17 Financial accounts differ from management accounts in that they:

A are prepared monthly for internal control purposes

B contain details of costs incurred in manufacturing

C are summarised and prepared mainly for external users of accounting information

D provide information to enable the trial balance to be prepared

18 Which of the following statements gives the best definition of the objective of accounting?

A To provide useful information to users

B To record, categorise and summarise financial transactions

C To calculate the taxation due to the government

D To calculate the amount of dividend to pay to the shareholders

EXPLAIN THE IMPACT OF THE REGULATORY FRAMEWORK ON FINANCIAL ACCOUNTING

19 Which organisation issues IFRS® Standards?

A The International Auditing and Assurance Standards Board (IAASB®)

B The Stock Exchange

C The International Accounting Standards Board (The Board)

D The Government

20 State whether each of the following statements are true or false.

	True	**False**
International accounting standards are effective only if adopted by national regulatory bodies.		
Accounting standards provide guidance on accounting for all types of transactions.		

RECORDING ACCOUNTING TRANSACTIONS

PREPARE ACCOUNTING RECORDS

21 RST had a cash balance of $1,000 on 1 June. During June, it sold goods on credit for $5,000 and made a profit of $1,000; it bought goods on credit for $2,000 and paid wages of $400.

What was RST's cash balance at 30 June?

$____________

22 **If an entity had an increase in receivables of $750, a decrease in the bank overdraft of $400, a decrease in payables of $3,000 and an increase in inventories of $2,000, what would be the change in working capital?**

increase/decrease of $____________

23 **The accounting equation can change as a result of certain transactions. Which one of the following transactions would not affect the accounting equation?**

A Selling goods for more than their cost

B Purchasing a non-current asset on credit

C The owner withdrawing cash

D Receivables paying their accounts in full, in cash

24 **If the owner of a business withdrew cash for personal use, what journal entry would record this transaction?**

A	Dr Capital	Cr Drawings
B	Dr Cash	Cr Drawings
C	Dr Drawings	Cr Capital
D	Dr Drawings	Cr Cash

25 **Goods withdrawn by a proprietor for personal use are entered into the accounting records as:**

A	Dr Drawings	Cr Purchases
B	Dr Purchases	Cr Drawings
C	Dr Capital	Cr Drawings
D	Dr Purchases	Cr Sales

26 **A credit balance of $1,834 brought down on BLT's account in the books of ABC means that**

A ABC owes BLT $1,834

B BLT owes ABC $1,834

C ABC has paid BLT $1,834

D ABC is owed $1,834 by BLT

27 Which one of the following statements is correct?

A Assets and liabilities normally have credit balances

B Liabilities and revenues normally have debit balances

C Assets and revenues normally have credit balances

D Assets and expenses normally have debit balances

28 On 1 January, a business had a customer, JKL, who owed $1,200. During January, JKL purchased further goods for $2,100 and returned goods valued at $750. JKL also paid $960 in cash towards the outstanding balance.

What was the balance of JKL's account on 31 January?

A $1,590 debit

B $1,590 credit

C $810 debit

D $810 credit

29 What accounting entries are required for ABC to record the return of office equipment that had been purchased on credit from PQR, but not yet paid for?

	Debit	**Credit**
A	Office equipment	Sales
B	Office equipment	PQR
C	PQR	Office equipment
D	Cash	Office equipment

30 Which one of the following statements relating to the balance on a ledger account is not correct?

A A credit balance exists when the total of credit entries is more than the total of debit entries

B A debit balance exists when the total of debit entries is less than the total of credit entries

C A credit balance exists when the total of debit entries is less than the total of credit entries

D A debit balance exists when the total of debit entries is more than the total of credit entries

31 Which of the following is the correct double-entry to record the purchase on credit of inventories intended for resale?

	Debit	**Credit**
A	Inventories	Receivable
B	Inventories	Payable
C	Purchases	Payable
D	Payable	Purchases

32 X purchases goods from Y on credit and X subsequently pays by cheque. X then discovers that the goods are faulty and cancels the cheque before it is cashed by Y.

How should X record the cancellation of the cheque in its accounting records?

	Debit	**Credit**
A	Payables	Returns outwards
B	Payables	Bank
C	Bank	Payables
D	Returns outwards	Payables

33 **When a transaction is credited to the correct purchase ledger account, but debited incorrectly to the repairs and renewals account instead of to the plant and machinery account, the error is known as an error of**

A omission

B commission

C principle

D original entry

34 An invoice from a supplier for office equipment has been debited to the stationery account.

What is the effect on profit and non-current assets?

	Profit		**Non-current assets**
A	Decrease	A	Decrease
B	Increase	B	Increase
C	No effect	C	No effect

35 DEF bought a machine for $15,000 on 1 January 20X1, which had an expected useful life of four years and an expected residual value of $3,000; the asset was to be depreciated on the straight-line basis. On 31 December 20X3, the machine was sold for $4,800.

What was the amount included in the 20X3 statement of profit or loss account for profit or loss on disposal?

$_______________

36 **Which of the following statements best defines depreciation in accordance with IAS 16 *Property, Plant and Equipment*?**

A It is a means of determining the decrease in market value of an asset over time

B It is a means of allocating the cost of an asset over a number of accounting periods

C It is a means of setting funds aside for the replacement of the asset

D It is a means of estimating the current value of the asset

37 A business purchased a machine for $120,000 on 1 January 20X3 and another one on 1 July 20X3 for $144,000. Depreciation is charged at 10% per annum on cost and calculated on a monthly basis.

What is the total depreciation charge for the two machines for the year ended 31 December 20X3?

A $13,200

B $19,200

C $21,600

D $26,400

38 **Which of the following statements is true in relation to the non-current asset register?**

A It is an alternative name for the non-current asset ledger account

B It is a list of the physical non-current assets, rather than their financial costs

C It is part of the double-entry bookkeeping system

D It is a schedule of the cost, date of purchase, location and other information for each individual non-current asset

39 **Which of the following items should be accounted for as capital expenditure?**

A Repairs to a forklift truck damaged after an accident in the warehouse

B The purchase of a vehicle for resale by a car dealer

C The cost of redecorating an office

D Legal fees incurred on the purchase of a building

40 EFG bought machinery for $300,000 on 1 January 20X5, and depreciated it at 10% per annum using the reducing balance method.

What was the depreciation charge for the year ended 31 December 20X7?

A $21,870

B $24,300

C $27,000

D $30,000

41 GHI business bought a machine for $72,000 on 1 January 20X0 and another machine for $96,000 on 1 July 20X0. Depreciation is calculated at the rate of 10% per annum on a straight-line basis, calculated on a monthly basis.

What is the total depreciation charge for the two machines for the year ended 31 December 20X0?

A $6,000

B $8,400

C $12,000

D $16,800

42 **In accordance with IAS 38 *Intangible Assets*, which of the following statements regarding goodwill is not correct?**

A Goodwill is classified as an intangible non-current asset

B Goodwill is the excess of the value of a business as a whole over the fair value of its separable net assets

C Purchased goodwill may be shown on the statement of financial position and is subject to regular impairment reviews

D Non-purchased goodwill is a liability

43 WXY Ltd purchases a new printing machine. The cost of the machine was $40,000. The installation costs were $2,500, and the employees received specific training on how to use this particular machine at a cost of $1,000. Before using the machine to print customers' orders, a test was undertaken, and the paper and ink cost was $500.

What should be the cost of the machine in the company's statement of financial position?

$___________

44 **The reducing-balance method of depreciating non-current assets is more appropriate than the straight-line method when**

A the expected life of the asset is short

B the asset is expected to decrease in value by a non-current percentage of cost each year

C the expected life of the asset cannot be estimated accurately

D it better reflects the pattern of the consumption of the economic benefits derived from the asset

45 **It is important to produce an opening trial balance prior to preparing the financial statements because**

A it confirms the accuracy of the ledger accounts

B it provides all the figures necessary to prepare the financial statements

C it shows that the ledger accounts contain debit and credit entries of an equal value

D it enables the accountant to calculate any adjustments required

46 **An error of original entry would occur if the purchase of goods for resale was**

A debited and credited to the correct accounts using the incorrect amount in both cases

B credited to the purchases account and debited to the supplier's account

C debited to a non-current assets account

D entered correctly in the purchases account, but entered in the supplier's account using the wrong amount

47 Which of the following statements best explains what a cash discount is?

A It is a discount for payments made in cash

B It is a discount for payments made by cheque

C It is a discount for payments made before the due date

D It is a discount for purchases made in bulk

48 How is a discount allowed to a credit customer accounted for in the financial statements?

A It is offset against discounts received in the statement of profit or loss

B It is a reduction in revenue in the statement of profit or loss

C It is an expense in the statement of profit or loss

D It is a liability in the statement of financial position

49 Where, in the financial statements, is the discount received classified?

A It is income in the statement of profit or loss

B It is offset against discounts allowed in the statement of profit or loss

C It is an asset in the statement of financial position

D It is disclosed in the statement of changes in equity

50 Which of the following statements best explains a trade discount?

A It is a discount granted by the seller to the purchaser for making purchases in bulk

B It is a discount granted by the seller when the customer pays in cash

C It is a discount granted by the seller for early settlement of the amount due

D it is a discount granted by the seller to overseas customers only

51 What is the double-entry to record a trade discount allowed to a customer?

A	Dr Revenue	Cr Trade discount
B	Dr Trade discount	Cr Revenue
C	Dr Purchases	Cr Trade discount
D	No double-entry is required	

52 How is carriage inward accounted for?

A It is an expense in the statement of profit or loss

B It is a liability in the statement of financial position

C It is income in the statement of profit or loss

D It is disclosed in the statement of changes in equity

53 The double-entry system of bookkeeping normally results in which of the following balances on the ledger accounts?

	Debit balances:	**Credit balances:**
A	Assets and revenues	Liabilities, capital and expenses
B	Revenue, capital and liabilities	Assets and expenses
C	Assets and expenses	Liabilities, capital and revenue
D	Assets, expenses and capital	Liabilities and revenue

54 What are the accounting entries required to record sales on credit of $10,000, on which sales tax is applied at the rate of 20%?

A Debit Trade receivables' control account $12,000, Credit Sales revenue $10,000 and Credit Sales tax $2,000

B Debit Trade receivables' control account $10,000, Credit Sales revenue $8,000 and Credit Sales tax $2,000

C Debit Sales revenue $10,000, Debit Sales tax $2,000 and Credit Suspense $12,000

D Debit Sales revenue $8,000, Debit Sales tax $2,000 and Credit Suspense $10,000

55 After calculating XYZ's profit for 20X9, you discover that:

- the purchase of goods for $3,400 had been included in a non-current asset ledger account, and
- interest received of $400 had been credited to sales.

State the amount by which gross profit and net profit respectively will change when the errors are corrected.

	Gross profit	**Net profit**
Increase/decrease	$__________	$__________

56 The cash book of BCD has a memorandum column to record settlement discounts when making early payment to suppliers. The column is totalled every week and posted to the nominal ledger.

What is the correct double entry in the nominal ledger?

A	Dr Cash	Cr Discounts received
B	Dr Cash	Cr Discounts allowed
C	Dr Trade payables	Cr Discounts received
D	Dr Discounts allowed	Cr Trade receivables

57 An entity received a settlement discount of $1,500 from a supplier. The amount was debited to the discount received account.

What was the effect of this transaction upon gross profit?

A Gross profit is understated by $1,500

B Gross profit is understated by $3,000

C Gross profit is overstated by $3,000

D Gross profit is unaffected

58 A book of prime entry is one in which:

A the rules of double-entry bookkeeping apply

B ledger accounts are maintained

C transactions are entered prior to being recorded in the ledger accounts

D subsidiary accounts are kept

59 A suspense account shows a credit balance of $260. Which of the following is a possible reason for the suspense account?

A Omitting a sale of $260 from the sales ledger

B Recording a purchase of $260 twice in the purchases account

C Failing to write off an irrecoverable debt of $260

D Recording an electricity bill paid of $130 by debiting the bank account and crediting the electricity account

60 A contra entry for $1,912 has been recorded in the accounting records, with the payables' ledger entry being in the account of Harry and the receivables' ledger entry being in the account of Carry. This contra, which should never have been made, is to be cancelled.

What will be the impact of the required correction?

	Purchase ledger control account	**List of supplier balances**
A	No effect	Increase total by $1,912
B	Credit $1,912	Increase total by $1,912
C	Debit $1,912	Decrease total by $1,912
D	No effect	Decrease total by $1,912

61 A total of $19,400 from the payments side of the cash book had been posted to the credit side of the payables' ledger control account.

What journal entry is required to correct this error?

	Debit	**Credit**
A	Payables' ledger control $19,400	Suspense account $19,400
B	Suspense account $19,400	Payables' ledger control $19,400
C	Payables' ledger control $38,800	Suspense account $38,800
D	Suspense account $38,800	Payables' ledger control $38,800

62 **A payment of $240 from petty cash for stationery had been entered in the books twice. What adjustment is required to correct this?**

	Debit	**Credit**
A	Stationery account $240	Suspense account $240
B	Stationery account $240	Petty cash $240
C	Suspense account $240	Stationery account $240
D	Petty cash $240	Stationery account $240

63 **Which of the following errors would cause an entry to be made in a suspense account?**

A Rent charges debited to the local business tax account

B Cash paid to a payable debited to the wrong payable's account

C Cash received from a receivable was debited to the wrong receivable's account

D Purchase of goods by the business for the proprietor's private consumption is debited to purchases

64 **The purchase of office equipment for $750 had been charged to the purchases account. What adjustment is required to correct this?**

	Debit	**Credit**
A	Office equipment account $750	Suspense account $750
B	Purchase account $750	Office equipment account $750
C	Suspense account $750	Purchase account $750
D	Office equipment account $750	Purchase account $750

65 Faulty goods returned by a customer with a sales value of $37 had been correctly treated in the customer's personal account and in the receivables' ledger control account, but had been credited to the sales returns account as $73.

What adjustment is required to correct this?

	Debit	**Credit**
A	Sales returns account $36	Suspense account $36
B	Suspense account $36	Sales returns account $36
C	Sales returns account $110	Suspense account $110
D	Suspense account $110	Sales returns account $110

66 Drag the correct word from the following list to complete each of the three statements relating to the identification of errors. Not all words have to be used and words can be used more than once.

- omission
- commission
- principle
- original entry

A An error where the wrong amount has been used for both the debit and credit entries is known as an error of ____________.

B An error of __________ is when the correct and incorrect accounts are of different types, for example, entered into a SOPL account instead of a SOFP account.

C An error where one side of the transaction has been entered in the wrong account (but of a similar type to the account and from the same financial statement) is known as an error of _____________.

67 After calculating your profit for the year ended 31 December 20X9, you discover the following errors:

- a purchase of inventory which had cost $15,000 had been included in the non-current asset account.
- an electricity bill for $10,000 had been included as rental income rather than as an electricity expense.

Drag and drop words and values from the available list to complete the following statement. Not all words have to be used and words can be used more than once.

These two errors had the effect of ________ gross profit by $________ and ________ net profit by ________.

Available words:

overstating/understating/$10,000/$15,000/$25,000/$35,000

68 Would each of the following errors require the use of a suspense account to balance the trial balance? Tick the appropriate box on the table for each error.

	Suspense account	**No suspense account**
The total of the sales book, $25,600, has been posted to the sales account as $26,500.		
The purchase of a motor van costing $15,000 has been debited to the purchases account instead of to the non-current asset account.		
The purchase of stationery on credit has been entered into both the stationery account and the payables account as $54 instead of $45.		
A charity donation of $50 from petty cash has not been entered into the petty cash book.		

69 **Drag and drop each of the transaction types listed below to match with the appropriate book of prime entry.**

- Credit sales
- Credit purchases
- Return of goods sold on credit
- Return of goods bought on credit
- Bank transactions
- Small cash transactions
- All transactions not recorded elsewhere

Book of prime entry	Transaction type
The journal	
Petty cash book	
Sales day book	
Purchases day book	
Cash book	
Sales returns day book	
Purchases returns day book	

70 **Drag and drop words and values from the available list to complete the following statement regarding a cheque transaction.**

When transacting business through a bank account using a cheque, the ________ makes out a cheque to the ________. The bank clearing system passes it to the drawer's bank for approval and payment, with the result that it is taken out of the drawer's bank account. This is known as ______________ for payment. Until the cheque is accepted by the drawer's bank, it is considered to be _________ and the bank has the right to return it as _______ if there is something amiss with it.

Available words:

dishonoured/un-cleared/drawer/payee/presenting a cheque

71 The bookkeeping system involves the use of books of prime entry.

Drag and drop the following transactions into the columns below to indicate the correct book of prime entry for each transaction.

- The write-off of irrecoverable debts
- The sale of goods for cash
- The sale of goods to a credit customer

Sales day book	Cash book	The Journal

72 Drag and drop the following elements into the boxes below to correctly state the accounting equation.

- Assets
- Equity
- Liabilities

[ ] = [ ] + [ ]

73 Complete the table of information below to present the accounting equation at the end of day 5.

Day 1 DEF commenced business, introducing $780 cash.

Day 2 Obtained a loan of $300 cash from a family friend.

Day 2 Purchased inventory for $1,000.

Day 3 Sold goods for $100 cash, which had cost $80 to purchase.

Day 4 Sold goods for $500 on credit, which had cost $400 to purchase.

Day 5 Bought a motor car for $1,000 on credit.

Assets	Equity	Liabilities
$	$	$

74 Tick the appropriate boxes in the table below to show in which financial statement each of the elements listed would be included.

Element	Statement of profit or loss	Statement of financial position
Assets	☐	☐
Liabilities	☐	☐
Expenses	☐	☐
Income	☐	☐
Equity	☐	☐

75 Tick the correct boxes in the table below to show whether each of the following transactions would require a debit or a credit entry.

	Debit	Credit
Increases in capital/equity	☐	☐
Increase in assets	☐	☐
Decreases in assets	☐	☐
Increases in income	☐	☐
Increases in expenses	☐	☐

76 Use the drop-down menu within the options below to show the correct debit and credit entry for each of the three transactions.

Transaction	Debit	Credit
Purchase of office equipment on credit for $890	Office equipment/Cash/ Payables/Loan/Purchases	Office equipment/Cash/ Payables/Loan/Purchases
Sale of inventory for $100 cash	Cash/Sales/Inventory Receivables	Cash/Sales/Inventory Receivables
Return of inventory that has been purchased on credit but not yet paid for	Purchases/Purchases returns/Inventory/Cash/ Payables	Purchases/Purchases returns/Inventory/Cash/ Payables

77 Use the drop down menu within the options below to show the correct debit and credit entry for the following transaction.

ABC purchased goods from DEF on credit. ABC paid for the goods within the agreed credit period of 30 days but subsequently discovered that the goods were not fit for purpose and cancelled the cheque payment before it was cashed by DEF.

How should ABC record the cancelled cheque?

Debit	Credit
Payables/Purchases returns/Bank/ Sales returns/Receivables	Payables/Purchases returns/Bank/ Sales returns/Receivables

78 Use the drop-down lists available to show the correct accounting entries arising from the totals in the cash payments book below, assuming that control accounts are part of the double-entry accounting system.

Date	Detail	Bank	Discount	Payables	Electricity	Stationery
		$	$	$	$	$
01.01.X7	XYZ Ltd	2,900	100	2,900		
05.01.X7	Admin office	1,000			1,000	
09.01.X7	Head office	500				500
15.01.X7	LMN Ltd	3,400		3,400		
20.01.X7	Head office	5,800			5,800	
		–––––	–––––	–––––	–––––	–––––
		13,600	100	6,300	6,800	500

Debit/Credit	Account	Value
Debit/Credit	Bank/Discount allowed/ Discount received/Payables/ Electricity/Stationery	$13,600
Debit/Credit	Bank/Discount allowed/ Discount received/Payables/ Electricity/Stationery	$100
Debit/Credit	Bank/Discount allowed/ Discount received/Payables/ Electricity/Stationery	$100
Debit/Credit	Bank/Discount allowed/ Discount received/Payables/ Electricity/Stationery	$6,300
Debit/Credit	Bank/Discount allowed/ Discount received/Payables/ Electricity/Stationery	$6,800
Debit/Credit	Bank/Discount allowed/ Discount received/Payables/ Electricity/Stationery	$500

79 ABC has an account in its nominal ledger for FGH, which has a debit balance of $1,089.

Drag and drop words from the list available to complete the following statement:

________ owes ________________ $1,089. In the ledger of FGH, this would represent the ________ balance.

Available words:

ABC/FGH/an asset/a liability

80 ABC has a customer, XYZ, who owed it $700 on the 1st of January. During January, XYZ purchased additional goods at a cost of $1,500 and returned some unwanted goods, which had cost $320. During January, XYZ also made a payment towards the settlement of its account of $750.

Drag and drop words from the list available to complete the following statement:

At 31st of January ABC's ledger accounts would include a ______ balance for XYZ for $______. This represents ______ to ABC.

Available words:

debit/credit/an asset/a liability/430/1880/1770/1130

81 **Tick the correct boxes in the table below to show whether the following non-current assets would be recognised as tangible or intangible non-current assets.**

	Tangible	**Intangible**
Land and buildings	☐	☐
Motor Vehicles	☐	☐
Goodwill	☐	☐
Machinery	☐	☐
Licences	☐	☐
Patents	☐	☐

82 **Tick the correct boxes in the table below to show whether each of the following items would be recognised as capital expenditure or revenue expenditure.**

	Capital expenditure	**Revenue expenditure**
Replacing a faulty part with a unit which is identical to the original unit.	☐	☐
Replacing a faulty part with a unit which has slightly increased production capacity.	☐	☐
Legal fees for the purchase of land.	☐	☐
Carriage costs for a replacement part for factory machinery.	☐	☐
Costs to build factory extension.	☐	☐

Repainting of the head office building exterior.	☐	☐

83 Drag and drop the correct options from the list below into the illustration below of all costs which can be capitalised when purchasing a non-current asset in accordance with IAS 16 *Property, Plant and Equipment*.

- Purchase price
- Delivery costs
- Legal fees
- Training costs
- Repairs and maintenance
- Subsequent expenditure that maintains the productive capacity of the asset
- Subsequent expenditure that enhances the productive capacity of the asset
- Trailing, testing and installation costs.

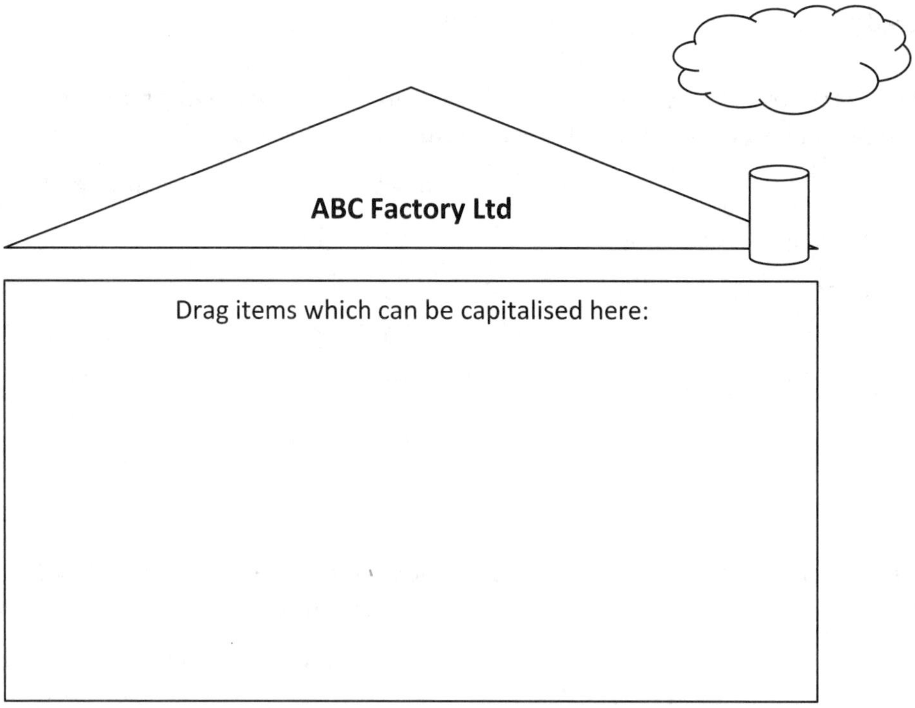

84 Drag and drop the correct options from the list below into the appropriate method of depreciation to fit the asset type.

Straight-line depreciation	Reducing-balance depreciation

- Useful for assets which provide equal benefit each year, e.g. machinery.
- Useful for assets which provide more benefit in earlier years, e.g. cars, IT equipment.

85 Drag and drop words and values from the available list to complete the following two statements regarding the disposal of a non-current asset.

If the proceeds received on disposal are less than the carrying amount at the date of sale, the difference is a ___________ which is treated as __________ when calculating the profit or loss for the year.

If the proceeds received on disposal are more than the carrying amount at the date of sale, the difference is a _____________ which is treated as ____________ when calculating the profit or loss for the year.

Available words:

profit on disposal/loss on disposal/an expense/income

86 Using the drop-down lists available, show the correct accounting entries at each stage of the process when accounting for the disposal of a non-current asset.

Step 1 – Remove the asset from the books.

Debit	Disposal account/Non-current asset account/ Cash account/Accumulated depreciation account
Credit	Disposal account/Non-current asset account/ Cash account/Accumulated depreciation account

Step 2 – Remove accumulated depreciation from the books.

Debit	Disposal account/Non-current asset account/ Cash account/Accumulated depreciation account
Credit	Disposal account/Non-current asset account/ Cash account/Accumulated depreciation account

Step 3 – Record the cash proceeds.

Debit	Disposal account/Non-current asset account/ Cash account/Accumulated depreciation account
Credit	Disposal account/Non-current asset account/ Cash account/Accumulated depreciation account

87 Using the drop-down lists available, show the correct accounting entries at each step of the process when accounting for the disposal of a non-current asset using a part exchange agreement.

Step 1 – Remove the asset from the books.

Debit	Disposal account/Non-current asset account/ Cash account/Accumulated depreciation account
Credit	Disposal account/Non-current asset account/ Cash account/Accumulated depreciation account

Step 2 – Remove accumulated depreciation from the books.

Debit	Disposal account/Non-current asset account/ Cash account/Accumulated depreciation account
Credit	Disposal account/Non-current asset account/ Cash account/Accumulated depreciation account

Step 3 – Record the part exchange value.

Debit	Disposal account/Non-current asset account/ Cash account/Accumulated depreciation account
Credit	Disposal account/Non-current asset account/ Cash account/Accumulated depreciation account

Step 4 – Record the remainder.

Debit	Disposal account/Non-current asset account/ Cash account/Accumulated depreciation account
Credit	Disposal account/Non-current asset account/ Cash account/Accumulated depreciation account

PREPARE ACCOUNTING RECONCILIATIONS

88 The petty-cash imprest is restored to $300 at the end of each week. The following amounts were paid out of petty cash during week 23:

Stationery	$42.30 including sales tax at 20%
Travelling costs	$76.50
Office refreshments	$38.70
Sundry payables	$72.00 plus sales tax at 20%

What is the amount required to restore the imprest to $300?

$___________

89 What effect on a positive cash balance does an adjustment for unpresented paid cheques have on a bank reconciliation?

A Increase in the cash book balance

B Decrease in the cash book balance

C Increase in the balance shown by the bank statement

D Decrease in the balance shown by the bank statement

90 The cash book shows a bank balance of $6,800 overdrawn at 31 July 20X9. It is subsequently discovered that a standing order for $300 has been entered twice, and that a dishonoured cheque for $750 has been debited in the cash book instead of credited.

What was the correct bank balance at that date?

$__________

91 ABC has just completed the following reconciliation of the bank statement to its cash book.

Bank reconciliation statement as at 31 December 20X5

	$
Balance as per bank statement	9,564
Add: Unpresented cheques	772
	10,336
Less: Uncleared lodgements	(218)
Balance as per cash book	10,118

What figure for cash should be included in the trial balance at 31 December 20X5?

A $9,564 Dr

B $9,564 Cr

C $10,118 Dr

D $10,118 Cr

92 A supplier sends you a statement showing a balance outstanding of $6,850. Your own records show a balance outstanding of $7,500. The reason for this difference could be that:

A the supplier sent an invoice for $650 that you have not yet received

B the supplier has allowed you $650 cash discount that you have not recorded in your accounting records

C you have paid the supplier $650 that they have not yet accounted for

D you have returned goods worth $650 that the supplier has not yet accounted for

93 Which of the following items would NOT lead to a difference between the trade receivables' ledger control account and the total of trade receivables' ledger balances?

A An error when totalling the sales day book

B An entry made in the wrong individual receivables ledger account

C An error when totalling the receipts column in the cash book

D Overstatement of an entry in an individual receivables ledger account

94 Your cash book shows a credit balance of $2,480 at 30 April 20X9. Upon comparison with the bank statement, you determine that there are unpresented cheques totalling $450, and a receipt of $140 that has not yet been passed through the bank account. The bank statement shows bank charges of $75 that have not been entered.

What was the balance on the bank statement?

$____________

95 An entity's cash book at 31 December 20X4 shows a debit balance of $2,125. When the bank statement is reviewed, it is identified that cheques drawn by the entity totalling $274 had not been presented. In addition, the statement recorded bank charges of $58, which had not been entered in the cash book.

What was the balance on the bank statement as at 31 December 20X4?

A $1,909 overdrawn balance

B $1,909 favourable balance

C $2,341 favourable balance

D $2,457 favourable balance

96 Tick the correct boxes in the table below to show the classification of the following differences between the bank statement and the cash book when performing a bank reconciliation.

	Unrecorded items	**Timing difference**	**Error**
Automated bank charges	☐	☐	☐
Unpresented cheques	☐	☐	☐
Interest received	☐	☐	☐
Dishonoured cheques	☐	☐	☐
Direct debits	☐	☐	☐
Uncleared lodgements	☐	☐	☐
Double charged account fee	☐	☐	☐

97 Using the drop-down lists available, show the correct accounting entries required when an entity transfers the daybook totals into the nominal ledger.

Transfer of the sales day book to the nominal ledger

Debit	SLCA/Sales/Purchases/PLCA/Cash/Bank/Sales ledger account
Credit	SLCA/Sales/Purchases/PLCA/Cash/Bank/Sales ledger account

Transfer of the purchases day book to the nominal ledger

Debit	SLCA/Sales/Purchases/PLCA/Cash/Bank/ Purchase ledger account
Credit	SLCA/Sales/Purchases/PLCA/Cash/Bank/ Purchase ledger account

98 Using the drop-down lists available, show the correct accounting entries arising from a contra entry

Debit	SLCA/Sales/Purchases/PLCA/Cash/Bank
Credit	SLCA/Sales/Purchases/PLCA/Cash/Bank

PREPARE ACCOUNTING ENTRIES FOR SPECIFIC TRANSACTIONS

99 Calculate the sales tax on $100 at a rate of 20%

A $20.00

B $16.67

C $120.00

D Nil

100 How much is the sales tax amount if the gross amount invoiced was $6,600, at a sales tax rate of 20%?

A $7,920

B $1,100

C $1,320

D $5,500

101 X purchased goods costing $500 from Z, which had a list price of $500 and which were subject to a trade discount of 20%. Z applies sales tax at the rate of 20% on all sales.

What was the net cost of the goods purchased?

A $480.00

B $400.00

C $600.00

D $333.33

102 X purchased goods costing $500 from Z, which had a list price of $5,000 and which were subject to a trade discount of 20%. Z applies sales tax at the rate of 20% on all sales.

How much sales tax was applied by Z on this transaction?

A $1,000

B $800

C $833.33

D $666.66

103 TYU purchased goods costing $500 from ZXY, which had a list price of $500, and on which were subject to a trade discount of 20%. ZXY applies sales tax at the rate of 20% on all sales.

What accounting entries should TYU make to record this transaction if it is registered to account for sales tax?

			$	$
A	Dr	Purchases	400	
	Dr	Sales tax	80	
	Cr	Payable		480
B	Dr	Payable	480	
	Cr	Sales tax		80
	Cr	Purchases		400
C	Dr	Purchases	600	
	Dr	Sales tax	100	
	Cr	Payable		700
D	Dr	Purchases	480	
	Dr	Sales tax	100	
	Cr	Payable		580

104 **The sales account is:**

A credited with the total of sales made, including sales tax

B credited with the total of sales made, excluding sales tax

C debited with the total of sales made, including sales tax

D debited with the total of sales made, excluding sales tax

105 An employee is paid at the rate of $20 per hour. Earnings of more than $300 a week are taxed at 20%. Employees' social security contribution is 8%, and the employer's social security contribution is 12%. During week 42, the employee works for 45 hours.

What amounts should be paid to the employee and included in the statement of profit or loss?

Paid to employee	**Statement of profit or loss**
$__________	$__________

106 The correct ledger entries needed to record the issue of 400,000 $1 shares at a premium of 60c, and paid for by cheque, in full, would be

	Debit	**Credit**
	$	$
Bank		
Share premium		
Share capital		

107 Drag and drop words and values from the available list to complete the following two statements relating to discounts.

________ are offered by an entity to its customers to increase the volume of sales made.

________ are offered to encourage credit customers to pay for items quicker than they have previously agreed to.

Available words:

Trade discounts/Cash discounts

108 Use the drop-down lists available to show the correct accounting entries to record the following transaction.

STU sold goods with a list price of $3,000 to WXY on a cash basis and allowed WXY a trade discount of 10%.

How should the transaction be recorded in the books of STU?

Debit	SLCA/Sales/Purchases/PLCA/Cash/Discounts Allowed	$3000/$2700/$3300
Credit	SLCA/Sales/Purchases/PLCA/Cash/Discounts Allowed	$3000/$2700/$3300

109 Using the drop-down lists available, show the correct accounting entries arising from the following transactions:

To record discounts allowed:

Debit	Revenue/SLCA/Sales/Purchases/PLCA/Discounts received/Cash
Credit	Revenue/SLCA/Sales/Purchases/PLCA/Discounts received/Cash

To record discounts received:

Debit	Revenue/SLCA/Sales/Purchases/PLCA/Discounts received/Cash
Credit	Revenue/SLCA/Sales/Purchases/PLCA/Discounts received/Cash

110 TUV purchased goods on credit at a cost of $5,000 and made sales of $4,900 on credit. TUV offers an early settlement discount of 3% to its customers if they pay within 7 days. TUV expect that customers will take advantage of the discount. TUV has been offered an early settlement discount of 2% on its purchases if it chooses to pay within 14 days.

TUV received payment from the customer within 7 days and also paid its supplier within the 14-day early settlement period.

Using the drop-down lists available, show the correct accounting entries for TUV to record the discount allowed and discount received based upon the available information.

On the sale transaction:

Debit	SLCA/Sales/Purchases/PLCA/Cash/Revenue/Discount received	$150/$100/$147/$98
Credit	SLCA/Sales/Purchases/PLCA/Cash/Revenue/Discount received	$150/$100/$147/$98

On the purchase transaction:

Debit	SLCA/Sales/Purchases/PLCA/Cash/Revenue/Discount received	$150/$100/$147/$98
Credit	SLCA/Sales/Purchases/PLCA/Cash/Revenue/Discount received	$150/$100/$147/$98

111 Using the drop-down lists available, show the correct accounting entries required at each stage of the process when accounting for payroll costs.

Step 1 – Gross wages expense

Debit	Gross wages expense/Wages payable/Employer SS expense/ SS and income tax payable/Cash paid
Credit	Gross wages expense/Wages payable/Employer SS expense/ SS and income tax payable/Cash paid

Step 2 – Accounting for employer SS obligation

Debit	Gross wages expense/Wages payable/Employer SS expense/ SS and income tax payable/Cash paid
Credit	Gross wages expense/Wages payable/Employer SS expense/ SS and income tax payable/Cash paid

Step 3 – Accounting for the employee's SS and Income tax obligation deducted from gross pay

Debit	Gross wages expense/Wages payable/Employer SS expense/ SS and income tax payable/Cash paid
Credit	Gross wages expense/Wages payable/Employer SS expense/ SS and income tax payable/Cash paid

Step 4 – Accounting for the net pay to employees

Debit	Gross wages expense/Wages payable/Employer SS expense/ SS and income tax payable/Cash paid
Credit	Gross wages expense/Wages payable/Employer SS expense/ SS and income tax payable/Cash paid

Step 5 – SS and Income tax paid to the tax authority

Debit	Gross wages expense/Wages payable/Employer SS expense/ SS and income tax payable/Cash paid
Credit	Gross wages expense/Wages payable/Employer SS expense/ SS and income tax payable/Cash paid

112 Using the drop-down lists available, show the correct accounting entries for the following pension contribution.

OPQ earns $1,000 gross in month 3 of the payroll year. Pension contributions have been agreed to be 7% of the monthly salary. The ledger entries to record the pension contribution are as follows:

Debit	Wages payable/Pension liability/Cash/Employer SS expense/SS and income tax payable	$70/$1,000
Credit	Wages payable/Pension liability/Cash/Employer SS expense/SS and income tax payable	$70/$1,000

113 An employee is paid a rate of $6 per hour. Earnings of more than $120 a week are taxed at 15%. Employees' SS contribution is fixed at 5%, and the employer's SS contribution is 7%. During the week ended, the employee worked for 37.5 hours.

Calculate the amounts to be charged to the statement of profit or loss and paid to the employee in the following scenario.

Statement of profit or loss	Paid to employee
$________	$________

114 Drag and drop words from the available list to complete the following three statements relating to the types of shares available.

________ entitles the holders to the remaining distributable profits at the discretion of the directors, after prior interests and claims have been settled.

________ entitles the holder to a fixed rate of dividend with an instrument which the entity has agreed to buy back from the shareholder at an agreed future date.

________ entitles the holder to a fixed rate of dividend which ranks ahead of ordinary shareholders for repayment of capital in the event of liquidation of the entity.

Available words:

Ordinary shares/Redeemable preference shares/Irredeemable preference shares

115 Drag and drop words from the available list to complete the following three statements relating to share capital terminology.

________ is that part of the authorised share capital that has actually been allotted to shareholders following their application for shares.

________ is that part of the issued share capital paid by shareholders plus any amount that they have agreed to pay in the future.

________ is that part of the called-up share capital which has been paid by shareholders at a specific date.

Available words:

Issued share capital/Called-up share capital/Paid up share capital

116 Use the drop down lists available to show the accounting entries to record the following share issue.

An entity issued 15,000 new ordinary shares with a nominal value of $1 each, at an issue price, in line with market price, of $4 each. The ledger entries to record this are as follows:

Debit	Bank/Share Capital/Share Premium	$15,000/$45,000/$60,000
Credit	Bank/Share Capital/Share Premium	$15,000/$45,000/$60,000
Credit	Bank/Share Capital/Share Premium	$15,000/$45,000/$60,000

117 Use the drop down lists available to show the accounting entries to record the following share issue.

An entity issued 10,000 new ordinary shares with a nominal value of $0.50 each, at an issue price of $2. The market price per share immediately prior to the share issue was $2.50. The ledger entries to record this are as follows:

Debit	Bank/Share Capital/Share Premium	$5,000/$15,000/$20,000/$25,000
Credit	Bank/Share Capital/Share Premium	$5,000/$15,000/$20,000/$25,000
Credit	Bank/Share Capital/Share Premium	$5,000/$15,000/$20,000/$25,000

118 Use the drop-down lists available to show the accounting entries to record the following share issue.

An entity issued 10,000 ordinary shares with a nominal value of $0.75 to its current shareholders free of any contribution from the shareholders. The market price per share immediately prior to the issue was $2. The ledger entries to record this transaction are as follows:

Debit	Bank/Share Capital/Share Premium	$7,500/$12,500/$20,000
Credit	Bank/Share Capital/Share Premium	$7,500/$12,500/$20,000

119 Tick the correct boxes in the table below to show which of the following would be recognised as advantages of either a bonus issue or a rights issue. Note – options can be ticked for more than one type of issue.

	Rights issue	**Bonus issue**
Shares are more marketable and more easily transferable due to their lower market value per share.	☐	☐
There is a better chance of the share issue being fully subscribed due to it having an issue price below the market price.	☐	☐
It is cheaper than an issue at the market price.	☐	☐

120 Drag and drop words from the available list to complete the following statement relating to reserves.

There are two types of reserves, capital reserves and revenue reserves. The difference between these is that capital reserves _______ be distributed as dividends. An example of a capital reserve would the _______ account.

Available words:

may/may not/share capital/retained earnings/share premium

PREPARATION OF ACCOUNTS FOR SINGLE ENTITIES

PREPARE ACCOUNTING ADJUSTMENTS

121 BCD paid rent on 1 October 20X2 for the year ended 30 September 20X3 of $600, and paid rent of $800 on 1 October 20X3 for the year ended 30 September 20X4.

What was the rent payable expense for the year ended 31 December 20X3?

$___________

122 NOP commenced business on 1 May 20X0 and is charged rent at the rate of $18,000 per annum.

During the period to 31 December 20X0, NOP made payments totalling $13,800 for rent.

What should the rent expense be in the statement of profit or loss for the accounting period to 31 December 20X0?

$___________

123 A decrease in the allowance for receivables would result in

A an increase in liabilities

B a decrease in working capital

C a decrease in net profit

D an increase in net profit

124 CDE measures inventory using the first in, first out (FIFO) basis. Opening inventory comprised 10 units at a cost of $4 per unit. During the accounting period, 30 units were purchased at a cost of $6, followed by issues of 12 units and a further 8 units.

What was the value of inventory at the end of the accounting period in accordance with IAS 2 *Inventories*?

$__________

125 As referenced in IAS 2 *Inventories*, in times of rising prices, the FIFO method of inventories valuation, when compared with the average cost method of inventories valuation, will usually produce

A a higher profit and lower closing inventory value

B a higher profit and a higher closing inventory value

C a lower profit and a lower closing inventory value

D a lower profit and a higher closing inventory value

126 Inventory movements for product X during the last quarter were as follows:

Opening inventories		6 items at $30.00 each
January	Purchases	10 items at $39.60 each
February	Sales	10 items at $60 each
March	Purchases	20 items at $49 each
	Sales	5 items at $60 each

If inventory is valued using the continuous weighted average cost method, in accordance with IAS 2 *Inventories*, what was the gross profit for the three months ended 31 March?

$__________

127 An entity uses the LIFO cost formula. Information regarding inventory movements during a particular month is as follows:

1	Opening balance	300 units valued at $3,000
10	Purchases	700 units for $8,400
14	Sales	400 units for $8,000
21	Purchases	600 units for $9,000
23	Sales	800 units for $17,600

What was the cost of closing inventories at the end of the month as per IAS 2 *Inventories*?

$__________

128 STU sells three products – Small, Medium and Large. The following information was available at the year-end:

	Small	**Medium**	**Large**
	$ per unit	$ per unit	$ per unit
Original cost	10	15	20
Estimated selling price	14	18	19
Selling and distribution costs	1	4	3
	Units	Units	Units
Units in inventories	300	400	600

In accordance with IAS 2, the value of inventories at the year-end should be:

$____________

129 ABC business had receivables of $1,950 at 1 January 20X3 and $1,200 at 31 December 20X3. $96,750 was received from customers on credit during the year.

Assuming that there were no irrecoverable debts and no discounts allowed, what were credit sales for the year?

A $96,000

B $96,750

C $97,200

D $97,950

130 LMN had receivables of $300 at 1 January 20X4 and $270 at 31 December 20X4. Credit sales amounted to $2,370, and cash received from receivables was $2,310; an irrecoverable debt of $30 was written off.

How much discount was allowed to customers during the year?

A $60

B $120

C $210

D $270

131 After the draft financial statements of CDE have been prepared, some inventories are found in an old shed, which was not included in the physical inventory count. It appears that they originally cost $1,000, but it was thought that they could be sold for only $100.

What was the effect on CDE's gross profit?

A Increase $100

B Decrease $900

C Increase $1,000

D Decrease $1,000

132 JKL received rent from occupiers of premises during 20X5 of $25,000. Of this, $1,600 related to the year ended 31 December 20X4 and $800 related to the year ended 31 December 20X6. At 31 December 20X5, there was rent due but not yet received on $500.

What was the rent receivable by JKL for the year ended 31 December 20X5?

$___________

133 An entity received and paid the following rent invoices during the year ended 31 December 20X7:

28 Feb	$1,380
31 May	$1,320
30 Aug	$1,170
30 Nov	$1,260

Additional information:

A rent invoice was received on 28 February 20X8 for $1,350, relating to the period 1 December 20X7 – 28 February 20X8.

Using the drop-down lists available, show the correct accounting entries for the year-end journal entry.

Debit	Rent expense/Accruals/ Prepayments/Bank	$1,350/$450/$900/$390
Credit	Rent expense/Accruals/ Prepayments/Bank	$1,350/$450/$900/$390

134 An entity received and paid the following rent invoices during the year ended 31 December 20X7:

1 Mar	$3,600
1 Jun	$3,600
1 Sept	$3,600
1 Dec	$4,500 (to cover period 1st Dec 20X7– 28th Feb 20X8)

The annual rental was increased to $18,000 per annum with effect from 1 December 20X7.

Using the drop-down lists available, show the correct accounting entries for the following year-end journal entry.

Debit	Rent expense/Accruals/ Prepayments/Bank	$4,500/$3,600/$1,500/$3,000/$2,400
Credit	Rent expense/Accruals/ Prepayments/Bank	$4,500/$3,600/$1,500/$3,000/$2,400

135 An entity rented out a property to a tenant, charging $1,500 per month for use of the property. During the year ended 31 December 20X4, the entity received $25,000 cash from the tenant.

Using the drop-down lists available, show the correct accounting entries for the following year-end journal entry.

Debit	Rent expense/Rental income/ Accrued income/Prepaid income/ Bank	$1,500/$2,083/$7,000/$18,000/ $25,000
Credit	Rent expense/Rental income/ Accrued income/Prepaid income/ Bank	$1,500/$2,083/$7,000/$18,000/ $25,000

136 **Drag and drop words from the available list to complete the following three statements regarding accounting concepts.**

The __________ concept reflects the idea that revenue earned during the accounting period is matched in the statement of profit or loss with the expenses incurred in earning that revenue.

The __________ concept states that we recognise revenue only when it's been earned, not necessarily when cash is received from the customer.

The _______ concept states that revenue and assets should not be recognised unless they can be measured reliably and it is probable that economic benefits will be received.

Available words:

accruals/realisation/prudence/going concern

137 **Drag and drop words from the available list to complete the following two statements regarding irrecoverable debts and allowance for receivables.**

____________ would be recognised when information comes to light to suggest that a customer is unwilling or unable to pay their debt in full, or even at all

_________ would be recognised when there is some doubt as to whether some of the entity's receivables may fail to pay their debts in full.

Available words:

An irrecoverable debt/An allowance for receivables

138 Using the drop-down lists available, show the correct accounting entries resulting from each step of the procedure when reversing a debt which had previously been written off.

Step 1 – Reinstate the debt

Debit	Receivables/Payables/Bank/Irrecoverable debts/ Allowance for receivable
Credit	Receivables/Payables/Bank/Irrecoverable debts/ Allowance for receivables

Step 2 – Recognise the payment

Debit	Receivables/Payables/Bank/Irrecoverable debts/ Allowance for receivables
Credit	Receivables/Payables/Bank/Irrecoverable debts/ Allowance for receivables

139 Input values and use the drop-downs provided to show the correct accounting entries arising at the end of December 20X3, given the following information.

The allowance for receivables for each year end was as follows:

31 December 20X1	\$5,500
31 December 20X2	\$8,250
31 December 20X3	\$10,000

Debit	Cash/Receivables/Allowance for receivables/ Irrecoverable debt expense	\$
Credit	Cash/Receivables/Allowance for receivables/ Irrecoverable debt expense	\$

140 Drag and drop words from the available list to complete the following statement relating to accounting concepts.

Accounting for irrecoverable debts and allowances for receivables represents an application of the ____________ concept. Trade receivables, as an asset in the statement of financial position should not be overstated.

Available words:

going concern/materiality/prudence/accruals

141 Drag and drop words from the available list to complete the following statements relating to accounting for inventory.

The carry forward of unused inventory is an application of the ____________ concept. This is an extension of the accruals concept.

Available words:

going concern/materiality/prudence/matching

142 Using the drop-down lists available, show the correct accounting entries required to recognise opening and closing inventory correctly in the financial statements.

Opening inventory brought forward from the previous year:

Debit	Cost of sales/Inventory asset /Bank/Sales/Purchases
Credit	Cost of sales/Inventory asset /Bank/Sales/Purchases

Closing inventory unused at the end of the accounting period:

Debit	Cost of sales/Inventory asset /Bank/Sales/Purchases
Credit	Cost of sales/Inventory asset /Bank/Sales/Purchases

143 Which of the following costs should be excluded from the cost of inventory? Select all that apply.

A Purchase price

B Delivery costs

C Production overheads

D Non-production overheads

E Storage costs

F Selling costs

144 Using the drop-down lists available in the table below, match the following inventory valuation methods to their key points as per IAS 2 *Inventories*.

Unit cost/ FIFO/LIFO/AVCO	The cost of the closing inventory is the cost of the most recent purchases of inventory.
Unit cost/ FIFO/LIFO/AVCO	Used when items of inventory are individually distinguishable and of high value.
Unit cost/ FIFO/LIFO/AVCO	The cost of closing inventory is the cost of the oldest remaining items purchased.
Unit cost/ FIFO/LIFO/AVCO	This method is used when the average cost can be calculated on a periodic and continuous basis.

145 Drag and drop words from the available list to complete the following two statements relating to the weighted average cost inventory valuation method.

________ weighted average cost is when an average cost per unit is calculated based upon the cost of the opening inventory plus the cost of all purchases made during the accounting period.

________ weighted average cost is when an updated average cost per unit is calculated following each purchase of goods. The cost of any subsequent sales are then accounted for at that weighted average cost per unit.

Available words:

Periodic/Continuous

The following information is provided for use for questions 146 – 148.

ABC has a closing inventory of 100 units at a cost of $4 per unit as of 31 December 20X4. During the first week of January 20X5, they entered into the following transactions:

Date	Transaction	Units	$ per unit	Total $
3rd January	Purchased	120 units	$4.50 per unit	$540
4th January	Purchased	200 units	$5.00 per unit	$1,000
6th January	Sold	280 units	$7.00 per unit	$1,960
7th January	Purchased	100 units	$5.50 per unit	$550

146 Calculate the value, as per IAS 2 *Inventories*, of the closing inventory at the end of the first week using the FIFO method of inventory valuation. (round to the nearest full $)

$___________

147 Calculate the value, as per IAS 2 *Inventories*, of the closing inventory at the end of the first week using the periodic weighted average cost method of inventory valuation? (round to the nearest full $)

$___________

148 Calculate the value, as per IAS 2 *Inventories*, of the closing inventory at the end of the first week using the continuous weighted average cost method of inventory valuation? (round to the nearest full $)

$___________

149 In accordance with IAS 2 in times of rising prices, which of the following will give a higher profit in comparison with the other methods?

A FIFO

B Periodic average cost

C Continuous average cost

D All are equal

The following information is provided for use for questions 150 – 151.

DEF uses the FIFO method to determine the value of its inventory. On 1 January, it had 20 units of inventory, which had cost $15 per unit. During the month of January, the following transactions took place.

Date	Transaction	Units	$ per unit	Total $
5th January	Purchased	50 units	$17.50	$875
14th January	Purchased	80 units	$18 per unit	$1,440
16th January	Sold	100 units	$25 per unit	$2,500
27th January	Purchased	50 units	$18.50 per unit	$925

150 What was the value of closing inventory at 31 January as per IAS 2 *Inventories*?

$__________

151 What was the cost of goods sold for January?

$__________

PREPARE MANUFACTURING ACCOUNTS

152 The following information relates to MNO for the year ended 31 March 20X4:

	$
Inventories at beginning of year	
Raw materials	20,000
Work-in-progress	4,000
Finished goods	68,000
Inventories at end of year	
Raw materials	22,000
Work-in-progress	8,000
Finished goods	60,000
Purchase of raw materials	100,000
Direct wages	80,000
Royalties on goods produced	6,000
Production overheads	120,000
Distribution costs	110,000
Administration expenses	140,000
Sales	600,000

What was MNO's cost of goods manufactured for the year ended 31 March 20X4?

$__________

153 If work-in-progress decreases during the period, then:

A prime cost will decrease

B prime cost will increase

C the factory cost of goods completed will decrease

D the factory cost of goods completed will increase

154 The cost of royalties paid on goods manufactured is included in:

A factory overheads

B selling and distribution expenses

C prime cost

D trading account

155 The prime cost of goods manufactured is the total of:

A all factory costs before adjusting for work-in-progress

B all factory costs of goods completed

C all materials and labour

D direct factory costs

156 Which one of the following costs would not be shown as a factory overhead in a manufacturing account?

A The cost of insurance on a factory

B The cost of an extension to a factory

C The cost of depreciation on a factory

D The cost of rent on a factory

PREPARE FINANCIAL STATEMENTS FOR A SINGLE ENTITY

157 Which one of the following is not part of the statement of profit or loss?

A Sales

B Gross profit

C Receivables

D Rent receivable

158 Which of the following items in the statement of financial position would change immediately following a bonus issue of shares?

A Equity share capital and cash

B Equity share capital and share premium

C Share premium and cash

D Share premium and retained earnings

159 Which one of the following items is not part of the statement of changes in equity?

A Issued share capital at the start of the accounting period

B Retained profit for the accounting period

C Non-current assets

D Revaluation surplus at the end of the accounting period

160 Which one of the following does not form part of the cost of goods sold?

A Closing inventories

B Sales

C Opening inventories

D Purchases

161 An entity had opening inventories of $400 and closing inventories of $2,000. During the year, it made purchases of $3,000 and made sales of $5,000.

What was the gross profit or loss for the accounting period?

A $3,600 Profit

B $400 Loss

C $10,400 Profit

D $4,400 Loss

162 An entity had a gross profit for the year of $4,300, and also had the following items included in its trial balance at the end of the year:

- Rent paid $1,000
- Interest paid $300
- Rent received $200

What was the entity's net profit for the year?

A $3,000 profit

B $3,200 profit

C $5,600 profit

D $5,800 profit

163 When comparing the most recent statement of financial position with that of the previous year, it was noted that inventories had increased by $500, payables had increased by $2,400, and the bank balance had decreased by $800. Receivables were unchanged.

What was the change in working capital?

A a decrease in working capital of $2,100

B an increase in working capital of $2,700

C a decrease in working capital of $2,700

D an increase in working capital of $2,100

164 Gross profit for the year ended 31 December 20X1 can be calculated from:

A purchases for 20X1 plus inventories at 31 December 20X1 less inventories at 1 January 20X1

B purchases for 20X1 less inventories at 31 December 20X1 plus inventories at 1 January 20X1

C cost of goods sold during 20X1 plus sales during 20X1

D net profit for 20X1 plus expenses for 20X1

165 What is meant by the term 'working capital'?

A Total assets less total liabilities

B Current assets less current liabilities

C Capital plus profit less drawings

D Capital plus profit less drawings plus non-current liabilities

166 BCD made sales of $24,000 during the month of January 20X1, incurred expenses of $12,000, and had a net profit of 10% of sales.

What was the cost of sales for January 20X1?

A $9,600

B $12,000

C $14,400

D $21,600

167 Revenue reserves are defined as:

A accumulated and undistributed profits of a company

B amounts that cannot be distributed as dividends

C amounts set aside out of profits to replace revenue items

D amounts set aside out of profits for a specific purpose

168 Which one of the following would you expect to find in the statement of changes in equity of a limited company, for the current year?

A Directors' remuneration

B Ordinary dividend proposed during the current year, but paid in the following year

C Loan interest payable

D Ordinary dividend proposed during the previous year, but paid in the current year

169 In a statement of profit or loss and other comprehensive income, the difference between 'profit for the year' and 'total comprehensive income for the year' is:

A Interest paid

B Income tax paid

C Revaluation surplus for the year

D Dividends paid in the year

170 Which one of the following items would you not expect to find in a statement of changes in equity?

A Dividends received

B Transfers between reserves

C Gains on revaluation of property

D Issue of shares

171 Revenue reserves would decrease if a company did which one of the following?

A Repaid a loan

B Transferred an amount into a 'General reserve'

C Issued shares at a premium

D Paid an equity dividend

172 LMN includes the following items as 'reserves' in its financial statements. Which one of them is wrongly classified?

A Retained earnings

B Allowance for receivables

C Revaluation surplus

D Share premium account

173 With reference to the statement of cash flows, which of the following statements is correct?

A Dividends declared are an outflow of cash under the heading 'financing activities'

B Dividends proposed are an outflow of cash under the heading 'financing activities'

C Dividends paid are an outflow of cash under the heading 'financing activities'

D Dividends paid are an outflow of cash under the heading 'investing activities'

174 Which one of the following is not a revenue reserve?

A Retained earnings

B General reserve

C A reserve to replace non-current assets

D Share premium

175 A statement of cash flows can best be described as:

A a statement showing the effects of profit on cash resources

B a statement of cash inflows and outflows from operating activities

C a statement showing the movement in working capital

D a statement showing the inflows and outflows of cash

176 Revenue reserves would increase if an entity:

A issued shares at a premium

B made a transfer from retained profit earnings to general reserves

C Increased retained earnings

D increased its bank balances

177 Based upon the following information, what was the cost of purchases for the accounting period?

	$
Opening payables	71,300
Cash paid to suppliers	271,150
Discounts received	6,600
Goods returned	13,750
Closing payables	68,900

$__________

178 Based upon the following information, what were the credit sales for 20X3?

	$
Receivables at 1 January 2003	30,000
Receivables at 31 December 2003	27,000
Total receipts during 2003 (including cash sales of $15,000)	255,000

$__________

179 Goods withdrawn by the owner for personal use should be recorded as:

A Debit Drawings, and Credit Purchases

B Debit Revenue, and Credit Drawings

C Debit Drawings, and Credit inventory

D Debit Inventory, and Credit Drawings

180 Revenue reserves would decrease if an entity:

A set aside profits to pay future dividends

B transferred amounts into 'general reserves'

C issued shares at a premium

D paid dividend

ANALYSIS OF FINANCIAL STATEMENTS

IDENTIFY INFORMATION PROVIDED BY ACCOUNTING RATIOS

181 Using the drop-down lists provided, choose the appropriate words from the available list to complete the following three statements relating to the return on capital employed ratio.

If an entity revalues its land and buildings, the value of the capital employed will increase/decrease.

If an entity has property, plant and equipment which is coming to the end of its expected useful life, this will result in an increase/decrease in ROCE.

If an entity invests in new property, plant and equipment, this will increase/decrease ROCE in the short term.

182 Using the table below, select from the drop-down lists to state whether each of the four scenarios would increase or decrease the gross profit margin.

Sales revenue over the years has remained stable, but costs have increased.	increase/decrease
Sales revenue and costs have both decreased, but costs by a greater proportion.	increase/decrease
There was a change in the sales mix, which resulted in a higher proportion of more profitable products being sold in the current year.	increase/decrease
The business won new trade discounts with key suppliers.	increase/decrease

183 Using the table below, select from the drop-down lists to state whether each of the four scenarios would increase, decrease or have no impact on average inventory days.

Operating a JIT inventory system.	increase/decrease/ no impact
Stockpiling inventory in preparation for a new sales drive.	increase/decrease/ no impact
Increasing sales in the year.	increase/decrease/ no impact
Negotiating new contracts with suppliers which include increased discounts.	increase/decrease/ no impact

CALCULATE BASIC ACCOUNTING RATIOS

184 If the selling price of a product was $700, and gross profit mark-up was 40%, what was the cost of the product?

$___________

185 What was the inventory turnover of an entity based upon the following information?

- Sales were $220,000
- Purchases were $160,000
- Opening inventories were $24,000
- Closing inventory was $20,000.

___________ times (to 1 decimal place)

186 The formula for calculating the rate of inventory turnover is:

A average inventories at cost divided by the cost of goods sold

B sales divided by average inventories at cost

C sales divided by average inventories at the selling price

D cost of goods sold divided by average inventories at cost

187 An entity's gearing ratio would increase if:

A the decrease in long-term loans is less than the decrease in shareholders' funds

B the decrease in long-term loans is more than the decrease in shareholders' funds

C interest rates increased

D interest rates reduced

188 BCD extracted the following information from its statement of financial position:

	$000
Inventory	3,800
Receivables	2,000
Bank overdraft	200
Payables	2,000

Calculate:

(a) the current ratio: _______:1 State your answer to 1 decimal place.

and

(b) the quick (acid test) ratio: _______:1 State your answer to 1 decimal place.

189 GHI provided the following information for the year ended 31 December 20X7:

Inventories at 1 January	$9,075
Inventories at 31 December	$4,500
Purchases	$36,325
Gross profit margin	30%

What was the GHI's gross profit for the year ended 31 December 20X7?

A $12,270

B $13,608

C $15,567

D $17,529

The following information is provided for use for questions 190 – 195.

The trading account of CDE for the year ended 30 June 20X5 is set out below:

	$	$
Sales		430,000
Opening inventories	50,000	
Purchases	312,500	
	362,500	
Closing inventories	(38,000)	
Cost of sales		(324,500)
Gross profit		105,500

The following balances have been extracted from CDE's statement of financial position at 30 June 20X5:

	$
Trade receivables	60,000
Prepayments	4,000
Cash in hand	6,000
Bank overdraft	8,000
Trade Payables	40,000
Accruals	3,000
Declared dividends	5,000

In questions 190 – 195 assume a year to comprise 365 days and ignore sales tax.

190 **Calculate the inventories days, using average inventories.**

______ days

191 **Calculate receivables days.**

______ days

192 Calculate payables days.

_______ days

193 Calculate the current ratio.

_______ :1 (to two decimal places)

194 Calculate the quick ratio (or acid test ratio).

_______ :1 (to two decimal places)

195 Calculate the length of the cash cycle in days.

_______ days

The following information is provided for use for questions 196 – 199.

The following information has been derived from the financial statements of OPQ for the year ended 31 December 20X5.

At 31 December 20X5

Current ratio	1.4:1
Quick ratio	0.9:1
Current assets minus current liabilities	\$32,000
Receivables collection period	6 weeks
For the year ended 31 December 20X5	
Operating profit for the year as a percentage	
of ordinary share capital in issue	40%
Annual rate of inventories turnover	8.775 times
Gross profit as a percentage of sales	25%

On 31 December 20X5 there were no current assets other than inventories, receivables and bank balances and no liabilities other than current liabilities. Assume a 52-week year.

---

196 Calculate the value of OPQ's current liabilities on 31 December 20X5.

$____________

197 Calculate the value of OPQ's inventories at 31 December 20X5.

$____________

198 Calculate OPQ's sales revenue for 20X5.

$____________

199 Calculate OPQ's bank balance at 31 December 20X5.

$____________

200 Which of the following transactions would result in an increase in capital employed?

A Selling inventories at a profit

B Writing off an irrecoverable debt

C Paying a payable in cash

D Increasing the bank overdraft to purchase a non-current asset

Section 2

ANSWERS TO OBJECTIVE TEST QUESTIONS

ACCOUNTING PRINCIPLES, CONCEPTS AND REGULATIONS

EXPLAIN THE PRINCIPLES AND CONCEPTS OF FINANCIAL ACCOUNTING

1 **A, B and D**

Depreciation is not an accounting convention; this is purely an application of IAS 16 *Property, Plant and Equipment*.

2 **B**

Capital maintenance is important for the measurement of profit because the concept states that a profit should not be recognised unless a business has at least maintained the amount of its net assets during an accounting period. Stated differently, this means that profit is essentially the increase in net assets during a period.

3 **B**

The accruals convention implies that the profits must be charged with expenses incurred, irrespective of whether or not an invoice has been received.

4 The historic cost convention **fails to take account of changing price levels over time**.

Transactions are normally included at their original cost to the business, but that does not preclude reductions in these figures for depreciation and other adjustments. The accounting profession has attempted to introduce systems of current cost accounting in the past, but these have never replaced the historical cost convention. Accounting transactions are always past transactions, but not necessarily using the historical cost convention.

5 In times of rising prices, the historical cost convention has the effect of ___**overstating**_____ profits and __**understating**_____ the statement of financial position asset values

6 **C**

The realisation principle, also known as the revenue recognition principle, refers to the application of the accruals concept when dealing with the recognition of revenue. This concept states that revenue can only be recognised when the underlying goods or services associated with the revenue have been delivered or rendered, respectively.

7 D

The capital maintenance concept states that a profit should not be recognised unless a business has at least maintained the amount of its net assets during an accounting period. Stated differently, this means that profit is essentially the increase in net assets during a period.

8 D

The going concern concept is the assumption that an entity will remain trading for the foreseeable future. This means that the entity will not be forced to liquidate or sell off its assets in the near future, and so assets should remain at their carrying values and not their enforced saleable value.

9 B, C and D

Stewardship is concerned with ensuring that there is a procedure in place to safeguard assets, provide properly for liabilities, protect against misuse of assets, and report adequately to the shareholders or stakeholders of the organisation.

10 B

Bookkeeping is the recording, categorising and summarising of financial transactions.

11

Change	No change
Wages being paid in cash	A payable being paid the amount due by cheque
	Raw materials being purchased on credit
	Non-current assets being purchased on credit

Transactions that affect only assets and liabilities do not affect capital. Profits increase capital and losses reduce capital.

12 D

Items A, B and C are all part of the bookkeeping system. D is the correct answer.

13 C

Profit can be calculated as the movement in capital over the course of the year, less any drawings.

14

Management accounting	Financial accounting
	Uses historical data
	Is a legal requirement
Uses both financial and non-financial information	
	Is normally prepared annually

15 A, C and D

The qualitative characteristics of the financial statements in line with the IASB Conceptual Framework are relevance, faithful representation, comparability, verifiability, timeliness and understandability.

16 Recording all transactions in the books of accounts is an aim of **financial** accounting.

Providing management with detailed analyses of costs is an aim of **management** accounting.

Presenting the financial results of the organisation by means of recognised statements is an aim of **financial** accounting.

Calculating profit is an aim of **financial** accounting.

17 C

Financial accounts are summarised as prepared mainly for external users. A, B and D are all features of management accounts.

18 A

The objective of accounting is to provide information which is useful to users. B, C and D are all uses of the financial statements, but they are not the objective.

EXPLAIN THE IMPACT OF THE REGULATORY FRAMEWORK ON FINANCIAL ACCOUNTING

19 C

The International Accounting Standards Board (IASB) issues **IFRS® Standards**.

20

	True	False
International accounting standards are effective only if adopted by national regulatory bodies.	✓	
Accounting standards provide guidance on accounting for all types of transactions.		✓

RECORDING ACCOUNTING TRANSACTIONS

PREPARE ACCOUNTING RECORDS

21 $600

The transactions on credit terms do not affect the cash balance.

22 Increase of $6,150

The effect on working capital is calculated as

	$
Increase in receivables = Increase in working capital	750
Decrease in bank overdraft = Increase in working capital	400
Decrease in payables = Increase in working capital	3,000
Increase in inventories = Increase in working capital	2,000
Overall increase in working capital	6,150

23 D

Receivables paying the accounts in full in cash would not impact the accounting equation as the transaction both increases and decreases the asset account. The effect is one of reducing receivables while increasing cash, and so the net effect on the accounting equation is nil.

24 D

The answer is not C because drawings will eventually be transferred to the capital account. The initial entry affects the drawings account.

25 A

Goods being withdrawn will be removed from purchases as they are not part of the resalable purchases, and the equivalent value will be shown as drawings instead. Debit to increase drawings and credit to decrease purchases.

26 A

A credit balance in the books of A Ltd indicates that it owes money; none of the distracters would result in a credit balance.

27 D

Assets and expenses normally have debit balances.

Liabilities and revenues normally have credit balances

28 A

= 1,200 (debit) + 2,100 (debit) – 750 (credit) – 960 (credit) = 1,590 debit

29 C

When purchased	**When returned**
Dr Office equipment	Dr PQR
Cr PQR	Cr Office equipment

30 B

If the total of the debit entries is less than the total of the credit balances, then this would reflect a credit balance, not a debit balance.

31 C

The inventories account is never used to record purchases.

32 C

To remove the cheque payment from the books to reflect the cancellation, X needs to reverse the original entry.

On payment of the cheque, X would have recorded a Dr to payables and a Cr to the bank. To reverse this entry, X should Dr Bank and Cr Payables.

33 C

This is a straightforward test of your knowledge of the types of errors that can exist. If the wrong account is used, and this results in an incorrect statement of profit, then an error of principle has been made. Debiting the repairs and renewals account results in an extra charge for expenses in the statement of profit or loss, when the item should be included as a non-current asset on the statement of financial position.

34 A, C

Profits: A Decrease

Non-current assets: C No effect

35 Loss of $1,200

The profit or loss on disposal is the difference between the carrying amount at the time of disposal and the disposal proceeds. An excess of disposal proceeds over carrying amount indicates a profit on disposal, while an excess of carrying amount over disposal proceeds indicates a loss on disposal.

The annual depreciation on the machine is calculated as:

$$\frac{\text{Cost} - \text{residual value}}{\text{Useful economic life}} = \frac{15{,}000 - 3{,}000}{4 \text{ years}} = \$3{,}000 \text{ per year}$$

Non-current asset disposal account

Cost	15,000	Accumulated depreciation	9,000
		Sale proceeds	4,800
		Loss	1,200
	15,000		15,000

36 B

Depreciation never provides a fund for the replacement of the asset, nor does it aim to show assets at their fair values.

37 B

	$
Machine 1: $120,000 × 10%	12,000
Machine 1: $144,000 × 10% × 6/12	7,200
	19,200

38 D

The non-current asset register is an itemised schedule of non-current assets that will include information for each asset, such as cost, date of purchase, location, serial or identification number, depreciation method and rate.

39 D

The only item that should be capitalised is the legal costs incurred on the purchase of a building. All of the remaining items are revenue expenses.

40 B

	$
Cost	300,000
Depreciation 10% 20X5	(30,000)
	270,000
Depreciation 10% 20X6	(27,000)
	243,000
Depreciation 10% 20X7	(24,300)

41 C

Machine 1: Cost 72,000 × 10% = 7,200

Machine 2: Cost 96,000 × 10% = 9,600 × 6/12 = 4,800

Total 7,200 + 4,800 = $12,000

42 D

A, B and C are correct in most situations. Non-purchased goodwill would not be recorded.

43 $43,000

	$
Cost of the machine	40,000
Installation	2,500
Testing	500
	43,000

44 D

The reducing balance method should be used to depreciate assets which have a reducing benefit over the course of their lives. This matches the reducing benefit with a reduced expense.

45 C

An opening trial balance will prove that the ledgers have equal debit and credit entries; it won't, however, prove accuracy because there could be errors contained that still allow the trial balance to balance. The opening trial balance does not give all the figures necessary because year-end adjustments still need to be processed.

46 A

An error of original entry occurs when an incorrect amount is posted to the correct accounts. This is the case in A only.

47 C

A cash discount is a discount for early settlement or prompt payment of an invoice.

48 B

A discount allowed is a reduction in revenue in the statement of profit or loss.

49 A

The discount received is a form of income and so would be recognised in the statement of profit or loss.

50 A

A trade discount is given as a reduction to the published list price of a product, usually to encourage customers to purchase bigger quantities and bulk buying.

51 D

No double entry is required – trade discount is already deducted from the initial amount at the point an invoice is prepared.

52 A

Carriage inwards is the cost of transporting goods purchased into the business.

53 C

Remember to include capital (equity) when considering ledger account balances.

54 A

	Ledger Account:	$
Debit	Trade receivables' ledger control account	12,000
Credit	Sales	10,000
Credit	Sales tax	2,000

55

	Gross profit	**Net profit**
Decrease	$3,800	$3,400

56 C

Discounts allowed by BCD's suppliers are discounts received in their records. A discount received is a form of income which reduces the amount payable. This would be recorded as a Dr to reduce payables and a Cr to discounts received to recognise the income on the statement of profit or loss.

57 D

The discount received is stated in the statement of profit or loss rather than the trading account; therefore, the net profit will be affected by $3,000, but the gross profit is not affected.

58 C

A is incorrect as the journal is one of the books of prime entry in which double-entry rules do apply. B is incorrect, as ledger accounts are not maintained in books of prime entry. D is incorrect, as subsidiary accounts are ledger accounts that are maintained outside the main ledgers.

59 B

A credit balance on the suspense account indicates that the debit total of the trial balance was higher than the credit total. An error that could cause this would involve either too great a value having been debited, too little a value having been credited, or a combination of these, where an item has been recorded as a debit when it ought to have been a credit.

A would result in too little having been debited to the customer's account

B would result in an additional debit entry; therefore, this is the correct answer

C would not cause any imbalance in the trial balance, as both the debit and credit entries will have been omitted

D would not cause any imbalance in the trial balance as both a debit and a credit entry have been made, even though they were the wrong way round

60 B

A contra entry is used to reduce receivables and payables. A contra entry should be recorded both in the nominal ledger and in the memorandum accounts. If the entry is to be reversed, then the effect will be to increase both the PLCA and the SLCA and to increase the list of balances for both customers and suppliers.

To increase the PLCA, there would be a credit entry of $1,912, and the supplier list of balances would be increased by $1,912.

61 C

This transaction should have been debited to the payables ledger control account. The incorrect credit entry would have resulted in a debit balance in the suspense account. To remove the incorrect entry to the payables ledger control account, a Dr of $19,400 and then a further Dr of $19,400 to post to correct the entry. Total debit entry to PLCA required is $38,800, and a matching Cr entry to suspense.

62 D

One of the entries needs to be removed. This is achieved with a Debit to petty cash and a Credit to stationery for $240.

63 C

A suspense account would be created when transactions are posted to the ledgers with unequal debits and credits. This would be the case in C, as the cash received should have been credited to the receivables account. A debit to the receivables account will have the result of a debit entry to both cash and receivables, and a suspense account would have been opened to balance the credit side.

64 D

This transaction should have been debited to the office equipment account, not to purchases. The incorrect entry should be removed from purchases with a Cr entry to purchases, then posted correctly into the office equipment account with a Dr entry to office equipment.

65 C

This transaction should have been debited to sales returns. The incorrect credit entry will have resulted in a suspense account being created. To remove the incorrect entry to sales returns, a Dr entry of $73 is required, and then to post the correct entry, a further Dr of $37 to sales returns. Total Dr entry to sales returns required is $110, and an equal entry Cr to the suspense account.

66 An error where the wrong amount has been used for both the debit and credit entries is known as an error of **original entry**.

An error of **principle** is when the correct and incorrect accounts are of different types, for example, entered into a SOPL account instead of a SOFP account.

An error where one side of the transaction has been entered in the wrong account (but of a similar type to the account and from the same financial statement) is known as an error of **commission**.

67 These two errors had the effect of **overstating** gross profit by **$15,000** and **overstating** net profit by **$35,000**.

68

	Suspense account	**No suspense account**
The total of the sales book, $25,600, has been posted to the sales account as $26,500.	✓	
The purchase of a motor van costing $15,000 has been debited to the purchases account instead of to the non-current asset account.		✓
The purchase of stationery on credit has been entered into both the stationery account and the payables account as $54 instead of $45.		✓
A charity donation of $50 from petty cash has not been entered into the petty cash book.		✓

69

Book of prime entry	**Transaction type**
The journal	All transactions not recorded elsewhere
Petty cash book	Small cash transactions
Sales day book	Credit sales
Purchases day book	Credit purchases
Cash book	Bank transactions
Sales returns day book	Return of goods sold on credit
Purchases returns day book	Return of goods bought on credit

70 When transacting business through a bank account using a cheque, the **drawer** makes out a cheque to the **payee**. The bank clearing system passes it to the drawer's bank for approval and payment, with the result that it is taken out of the drawer's bank account. This is known as **presenting a cheque** for payment. Until the cheque is accepted by the drawer's bank, it is considered to be **un-cleared** and the bank has the right to return it as **dishonoured** if there is something amiss with it.

71

Sales day book	Cash book	The Journal
The sale of goods to a credit customer	The sale of goods for cash	The write-off of irrecoverable debts

72

Assets = Equity + Liabilities

73

Assets	Equity	Liabilities
$2,200	**$900**	**$1,300**

74

Element	**Statement of profit or loss**	**Statement of financial position**
Assets	☐	☑
Liabilities	☐	☑
Expenses	☑	☐
Income	☑	☐
Equity	☐	☑

75

	Debit	**Credit**
Increases in capital/equity	☐	☑
Increase in assets	☑	☐
Decreases in assets	☐	☑
Increases in income	☐	☑
Increases in expenses	☑	☐

76

Transaction	Debit	Credit
Purchase of office equipment on credit for $890	Office equipment	Payables
Sale of inventory for $100 cash	Cash	Sales
Return of inventory that has been purchased on credit but not yet paid for	Payables	Purchases returns

77

Debit	Credit
Bank	Payables

Note: ABC would record the return of goods as: Debit Payables and Credit Returns Outwards.

78

Debit/Credit	Account	Value
Credit	Bank	$13,600
Debit	Payables	$100
Credit	Discount received	$100
Debit	Payables	$6,300
Debit	Electricity	$6,800
Debit	Stationery	$500

79 **FGH** owes **ABC** $1,089. In the ledger of FGH, this would represent **a liability** balance.

80 At 31 January, ABC's ledger accounts would include a debit balance for XYZ of $1,130. This represents an asset to ABC.

81

	Tangible	Intangible
Land and buildings	☑	☐
Motor Vehicles	☑	☐
Goodwill	☐	☑
Machinery	☑	☐
Licences	☐	☑
Patents	☐	☑

82

	Capital expenditure	Revenue expenditure
Replacing a faulty part with a unit which is identical to the original unit.	☐	☑
Replacing a faulty part with a unit which has slightly increased production capacity.	☑	☐
Legal fees for the purchase of land.	☑	☐
Carriage costs for a replacement part for factory machinery.	☐	☑
Costs to build factory extension.	☑	☐
Repainting of the head office building exterior.	☐	☑

83

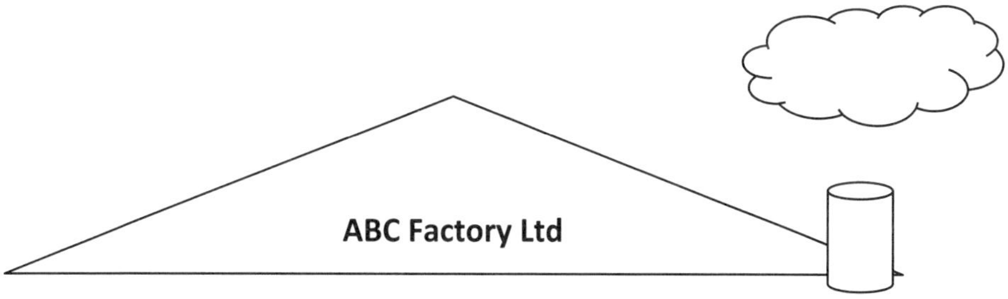

Drag items which can be capitalised here:

- Purchase price
- Delivery costs
- Legal fees
- Subsequent expenditure that enhances the productive capacity of the asset
- Trialling, testing and installation costs.

84

Straight-line depreciation	Reducing-balance depreciation
• Useful for assets which provide equal benefit each year, e.g. machinery.	• Useful for assets which provide more benefit in earlier years, e.g. cars, IT equipment.

85 If the proceeds received on disposal are less than the carrying amount at the date of sale, the difference is a **loss on disposal,** which is treated as **an expense** when calculating the profit or loss for the year.

If the proceeds received on disposal are more than the carrying amount at the date of sale, the difference is a profit on disposal, which is treated as **income** when calculating the profit or loss for the year.

86

Step 1 – Remove the asset from the books.

Debit	Disposal account
Credit	Non-current asset account

Step 2 – Remove accumulated depreciation from the books.

Debit	Accumulated depreciation account
Credit	Disposal account

Step 3 – Record the cash proceeds.

Debit	Cash account
Credit	Disposal account

87

Step 1 – Remove the asset from the books.

Debit	Disposal account
Credit	Non-current asset account

Step 2 – Remove accumulated depreciation from the books.

Debit	Accumulated depreciation account
Credit	Disposal account

Step 3 – Record the part exchange value.

Debit	Non-current asset account
Credit	Disposal account

Step 4 – Record the remainder.

Debit	Non-current asset account
Credit	Cash account

PREPARE ACCOUNTING RECONCILIATIONS

88 $243.90

	$
Stationery	42.30
Travelling cost	76.50
Refreshments	38.70
Sundry payables ($72.00 × 1.2)	86.40
	243.90 to restore to 300

89 D

Unpresented cheques have been recorded correctly as a reduction in the cash book, but since they have not yet been presented by suppliers to the bank, the bank statement is overstated; to reconcile this difference, a decrease in the balance shown on the bank statement is required.

90 $8,000 Overdrawn

(6,800) + 300 – (750 × 2) = (8,000)

91 D

The nature of the reconciliation indicates that ABC has an overdraft. For example, unpresented cheques have an adverse effect on the bank balance, here they are increasing therefore the bank account is overdrawn.

92 B

If the supplier believes that we owe less than we have recorded on our own ledgers, this could be the result of them offering us a discount which we have not entered into our records. This would be recorded as a discount received in your accounting records.

A, C and D would result in them having a higher balance owing than we are showing in our records.

93 B

All other items would result in an error in either the total of the trade receivables' ledger control account, or an error in the total of the receivables' ledger balances. Item B will result in errors to two individual receivables' ledger account balances; one will be overstated and the other understated by the same amount.

94 $2,245 Overdrawn

	$
Cash book balance	(2,480)
Unpresented cheques	450
Receipt not yet processed	(140)
Bank charges	(75)
As per statement	(2,245)

95 C

2,125 + 274 – 58 = 2,341

96

	Unrecorded items	Timing difference	Error
Automated bank charges	☑	☐	☐
Unpresented cheques	☐	☑	☐
Interest received	☑	☐	☐
Dishonoured cheques	☑	☐	☐
Direct debits	☑	☐	☐
Uncleared lodgements	☐	☑	☐
Double charged account fee	☐	☐	☑

97 Transfer of the sales day book to the nominal ledger

Debit	SLCA
Credit	Sales

Transfer of the purchases day book to the nominal leger

Debit	Purchases
Credit	PLCA

98

Debit	PLCA
Credit	SLCA

PREPARE ACCOUNTING ENTRIES FOR SPECIFIC TRANSACTIONS

99 A

$100 × 20% = $20

100 B

$6,600 × 20/120 = $1,100

101 B

	$
List price	500
Less: Trade discount	(100)
Purchases	400

102 B

	$
List price	5,000.00
Less: Trade discount	(1,000.00)
Net purchases	4,000.00
Sales tax @ 20%	800.00
	4,800.00

103 A

		$	$
Dr	Purchases	400	
Dr	Sales tax	80	
Cr	Payable		480

104 B

Sales tax is excluded from sales and purchases accounts, so items A and C are incorrect. Sales are a category of revenue, and therefore, the sales account is credited.

105 $708 and $1,008

	Hours		$
Gross pay	$20	45	900
Tax		900	
Threshold		(300)	
	20%	600	(120)
Employee SS	8%	900	(72)
Paid to the employee			**708**
Wages IS			900
Employer SS	12%	900	108
Statement of profit or loss charge			**1,008**

106

	Debit	Credit
Bank	640,000	
Share premium		240,000
Share capital		400,000

107 **Trade discounts** are offered by an entity to its customers to increase the volume of sales made.

Cash discounts are offered to encourage credit customers to pay for items quicker than they have previously agreed to.

108

Debit	Cash	$2,700
Credit	Sales	$2,700

109

To record discounts allowed:

Debit	Revenue
Credit	SLCA

To record discounts received:

Debit	PLCA
Credit	Discounts received

110

Sale transaction:

Debit	Revenue ($4,900 × 3%)	$147
Credit	SLCA	$147

Purchase transaction:

Debit	PLCA	$100
Credit	Discount received ($5,000 × 2%)	$100

111

Step 1 – Gross wages expense

Debit	Gross wages expense
Credit	Wages payable

Step 2 – Accounting for employer SS obligation

Debit	Employer SS expense
Credit	SS and income tax payable

Step 3 – Accounting for the employee's SS and Income tax obligation deducted from gross pay

Debit	Wages payable
Credit	SS and income tax payable

Step 4 – Accounting for the net pay to employees

Debit	Wages payable
Credit	Cash paid

Step 5 – SS and Income tax paid to the tax authority

Debit	SS and income tax payable
Credit	Cash paid

112

Debit	Wages payable	$70
Credit	Pension liability	$70

113

Statement of profit or loss	Paid to the employee
$15.75 + $225 = $240.75	$225 – $11.25 – $15.75 = $198

114 **Ordinary shares** entitle the holders to the remaining distributable profits at the discretion of the directors, after prior interests and claims have been settled.

Redeemable preference shares entitle the holder to a fixed rate of dividend with an instrument which the entity has agreed to buy back from the shareholder at an agreed future date.

Irredeemable preference shares entitle the holder to a fixed rate of dividend, which ranks ahead of ordinary shareholders for repayment of capital in the event of liquidation of the entity.

115 **Issued share capital** is that part of the authorised share capital that has actually been allotted to shareholders following their application for shares.

Called-up share capital is that part of the issued share capital paid by shareholders, plus any amount that they have agreed to pay in the future.

Paid-up share capital is that part of the called-up share capital which has been paid by shareholders at a specific date.

116

Debit	Bank	$60,000
Credit	Share Capital	$15,000
Credit	Share Premium	$45,000

117

Debit	Bank	$20,000
Credit	Share Capital	$5,000
Credit	Share Premium	$15,000

118

Debit	Share Premium	$7,500
Credit	Share Capital	$7,500

119

	Rights issue	**Bonus issue**
Shares are more marketable and more easily transferable due to their lower market value per share.	☑	☑
There is a better chance of the share issue being fully subscribed due to it having an issue price below the market price.	☑	☐
It is cheaper than an issue at the market price.	☑	☑

120 There are two types of reserves, capital reserves and revenue reserves. The difference between these is that capital reserves may not be distributed as dividends. An example of a capital reserve would be the share premium account.

PREPARATION OF ACCOUNTS FOR SINGLE ENTITIES

PREPARE ACCOUNTING ADJUSTMENTS

121 $650

The year to 31 December 20X3 includes 3/4 of the rent for the year to 30 September 20X3 and 1/4 of the rent for the year to 30 September 20X4, that is:

(3/4 × $600) + (1/4 × $800) = $650

122 $12,000

(8/12 × $18,000) = $12,000

123 D

The change in allowance for receivables is taken to the statement of profit or loss – an increase is debited and therefore decreases net profit, whilst a decrease is credited and therefore increases net profit. The resulting balance on the allowance for receivables account is deducted from receivables (current assets), which in turn affects working capital. A decrease in the allowance would increase net profit and would increase current assets. The latter is not one of the options; therefore, D is the answer.

124 $120.00

Closing inventory = 10 + 30 – 12 – 8 = 20 units, each valued at a cost of $6.00.

125 B

The closing inventories figure reduces the cost of goods sold figure, which in turn increases the gross profit.

Therefore, a higher closing inventories figure means a lower cost of goods sold figure, and hence a higher gross profit. In times of rising prices, the FIFO method of inventory valuation will produce higher closing inventory values and, therefore, higher gross profit figures.

126 $310

Summarised inventory card

	Quantity	Value ($)	
6 × $30	6	180	
10 × $39.60	10	396	
	16	576	($36 each)
10 × $36	(10)	(360)	
	6	216	
20 × $49	20	980	
	26	1,196	($46 each)
5 × $46	(5)	(230)	
	21	966	

Note: Issues are shown in brackets.

Trading account

	$	$
Sales (15 × $60)		900
Opening inventories	180	
Add: Purchases (396 + 980)	1,376	
	1,556	
Less: Closing inventories	(966)	
		(590)
Profit		310

127 $4,200

Closing inventory = 300 + 700 – 400 + 600 – 800 = 400 units. They are valued as follows: 300 units at $10 = $3,000 plus 100 units at $12 = $1,200, giving a total valuation of $4,200.

128 $18,200

Lower of cost and net realisable value

	Units	$	$
Small	300	10	3,000
Medium	400	14	5,600
Large	600	16	9,600
			18,200

129 A

Receivables control

	$		$
Bal b/d	1,950	Cash	96,750
Sales (Balancing figure)	96,000	Bal c/d	1,200
	97,950		97,950

130 A

Receivables control

	$		$
Bal b/d	300	Cash	2,310
Sales	2,370	Irrecoverable debts written off	30
		Discount allowed (bal. fig.)	60
		Bal c/d	270
	2,670		2,670

131 A

Omitted from closing inventories, therefore its inclusion will increase profit by the lower of cost and net realisable value, i.e. $100.

132 $23, 100

Rent receivable

	$		$
Bal b/f	1,600	Cash received	25,000
Profit or loss	23,100		
Balance c/f	800	Balance c/f	500
	25,500		25,500

133

Debit	Rent expense	$450
Credit	Accruals	$450

134

Debit	Prepayments	$3,000
Credit	Rent	$3,000

135

Debit	Rental income	$7,000
Credit	Prepaid income	$7,000

136 The **accruals** concept reflects the idea that revenue earned during the accounting period is matched in the statement of profit or loss with the expenses incurred in earning that revenue.

The **realisation** concept states that we recognise revenue only when it's been earned, not necessarily when cash is received from the customer.

The **prudence** concept states that revenue and assets should not be recognised unless they can be measured reliably and it is probable that economic benefits will be received.

137 **An irrecoverable debt** would be recognised when information comes to light to suggest that a customer is unwilling or unable to pay their debt in full, or even at all

An allowance for receivables would be recognised when there is some doubt as to whether some of the entity's receivables may fail to pay their debts in full.

138

Step 1 – Reinstate the debt

Debit	Receivables
Credit	Irrecoverable debts

Step 2 – Recognise the payment

Debit	Bank
Credit	Receivables

139

Debit	Irrecoverable debt expense	$1,750
Credit	Allowance for receivables	$1,750

140 Accounting for irrecoverable debts and allowances for receivables represents an application of the **prudence** concept. Trade receivables, as an asset in the statement of financial position, should not be overstated.

141 The carry forward of unused inventory is an application of the **matching** concept. This is an extension of the accruals concept.

142

Opening inventory brought forward from the previous year:

Debit	Cost of sales
Credit	Inventory asset

Closing inventory unused at the end of the accounting period:

Debit	Inventory asset
Credit	Cost of sales

143 D, E and F

In accordance with IAS 2, costs included within the cost of inventory include all costs incurred in bringing the inventories to their present location and condition, including the cost of purchase and conversion. The conversion costs would include only direct production costs.

D is a non-production cost.

E and F are both post-conversion.

144

FIFO	The cost of the closing inventory is the cost of the most recent purchases of inventory.
Unit cost	Used when items of inventory are individually distinguishable and of high value.
LIFO	The cost of closing inventory is the cost of the oldest remaining items purchased.
AVCO	This method is used when the average cost can be calculated on a periodic and continuous basis.

145 **Periodic** weighted average cost is when an average cost per unit is calculated based upon the cost of the opening inventory plus the cost of all purchases made during the accounting period.

Continuous weighted average cost is when an updated average cost per unit is calculated following each purchase of goods. The cost of any subsequent sales are then accounted for at that weighted average cost per unit.

146 $1,250

Date	Transaction	Units	$ per unit	Total $	Issues	Inventory
1st January	Opening inventory	100	$4.00 per unit	$400		
3rd January	Purchased	120 units	$4.50 per unit	$540		
4th January	Purchased	200 units	$5.00 per unit	$1,000		
6th January	Sold	280 units	$7.00 per unit	$1,960	100 @ 4.00 = $400 120 @ $4.50 = $540 60 @ $5.00 = $300 Total = $1,240	140 @ $5.00 = $700
7th January	Purchased	100 units	$5.50 per unit	$550		140 @ $5.00 = $700 100 @ $5.50 = $550 Total = $1,250

147 $1,150

Periodic average = (100 × $4.00) + (120 × $4.50) + (200 × $5.00) + (100 × $5.50)/(100 + 120 + 200 + 100) = $4.79 per unit.

Closing inventory = 100 + 120 + 200 – 280 + 100 = 240 units

Closing inventory valuation = 240 units × $4.79 = $1,150

148 $1,195

Date	Transaction	Units	$ per unit	Total $	Average per unit	Issue	Closing Inv
1st January	Opening inventory	100	$4.00 per unit	$400	$4.00		
3rd January	Purchased	120 units	$4.50 per unit	$540	$4.27		
4th January	Purchased	200 units	$5.00 per unit	$1,000	$4.62		
6th January	Sold	280 units	$7.00 per unit	$1,960		280 @ $4.62 = $1,294	140 @ $4.62 = $646
7th January	Purchased	100 units	$5.50 per unit	$550	$4.98		240 @ 4.98 = $1,195

149 A

In time of rising prices FIFO will always give a higher profit as it removes the older items from inventory first leaving closing inventory with the higher cost inventory remaining. The higher figure for closing inventory will give a reduced cost of sale and result in a higher profit overall.

150 $1,825

Date	Transaction	Units	$ per unit	Closing Inv $
1st January	Opening inventory	20	$15	$300
5th January	Purchased	50 units	$17.50	20 @ $15 = $300 + 50 @ $17.50 = $875 Total = $1,175
14th January	Purchased	80 units	$18 per unit	20 @ $15 = $300 + 50 @ $17.50 = $875 + 80 @ $18 = $1,440 Total = $2,615
16th January	Sold	100 units	$25 per unit	50 @ $18 = $900
27th January	Purchased	50 units	$18.50 per unit	50 @ $18 = $900 + 50 @ $18.50 = $925 total = $1,825

151 $1,715

	Opening inventory	$300
+	purchases ($875 + $1,440 + $925)	$3,240
–	Closing inventory	($1,825)
	Cost of goods sold	$1,715

PREPARE MANUFACTURING ACCOUNTS

152 $300,000

Cost of goods manufactured is found as follows:

	$
Opening inventories of raw materials	20,000
Purchases of raw materials	100,000
Less: Closing inventories of raw materials	(22,000)
	98,000
Direct wages	80,000
Royalties on goods produced	6,000
Prime cost	184,000
Production overheads	120,000
	304,000
Less: Increase in work-in-progress	(4,000)
Cost of goods manufactured	300,000

153 D

A decrease in work-in-progress means fewer goods are partly complete, thus the value of completed goods will be higher.

154 C

Royalties paid on production are a direct expense and are therefore part of prime cost.

155 D

The prime cost of goods manufactured in the total of direct factory costs.

156 B

The cost of an extension to a factory is a capital expenditure and would be shown as an asset in the statement of financial position.

PREPARE FINANCIAL STATEMENTS FOR A SINGLE ENTITY

157 C

Receivables are an asset, and so part of the statement of financial position.

158 B

Equity share capital is increased and share premium is reduced when a bonus issue is made.

159 C

Non-current assets are included in the statement of financial position.

160 B

Cost of goods sold is calculated as opening inventory + purchases – closing inventory. Sales are not included in the calculation.

161 A

	$	$
Sales		5,000
Less Cost of Sales		
Opening inventories	400	
+ Purchases	3,000	
– Closing inventories	(2,000)	(1,400)
Gross Profit		3,600

162 B

	$
Gross Profit	4,300
+ Rent received	200
– Rent paid	(1,000)
– Interest paid	(300)
Net Profit	3,200

163 C

	$
Increase in inventories = Increase in working capital	500
Decrease in bank = Decrease in working capital	(800)
Increase in payable = Decrease in working capital	(2,400)
Overall decrease in working capital	(2,700)

164 D

Working backwards often confuses candidates. Try drawing up a short example of a statement of profit or loss using simple figures of your own, to prove or disprove the options given – e.g.

	$	$
Sales		20,000
Inventories at 31.12.2000	2,000	
Add: Purchases during 2001	8,000	
	10,000	
Less: Inventories at 31.12.2001	(1,000)	
Cost of goods sold		(9,000)
Gross profit		11,000
Less: expenses		4,000
Profit for the period		7,000

Make all the figures different or you will make mistakes.

You can now see the options A, B and C will not give the correct answer.

165 B

Working capital is the total of current assets less current liabilities.

166 A

	$
Sales	24,000
COS (bal fig 2)	(9,600)
Gross profit (bal fig 1)	14,400
Indirect expenses	(12,000)
Profit for the period (10% × 24,000)	2,400

167 A

Revenue reserves can be distributed as dividends, so B is incorrect. Revenue reserves are not set aside to replace revenue items; they could be set aside for a specific purpose but this is only one use of revenue reserves.

168 D

Dividends proposed are not shown in the statement of changes in equity. Directors' and auditors' fees are normal business expenses and appear in the statement of profit or loss and other comprehensive income.

169 C

Total comprehensive income includes the profit for the year as well as any unrealised gains or losses such as a revaluation surplus in the year.

170 A

This item is included in the statement of profit or loss for the year.

171 D

A reserve is a component of equity. Repayment of a loan is a reduction in liabilities.

172 B

The allowance for receivables is technically a liability and not a reserve; it would be shown on the statement of financial position netted off against receivables within current assets.

173 C

Dividends paid would be shown on the statement of cash flows, not dividends declared or proposed. Dividends paid are part of financing activities.

174 D

Share premium is a capital reserve created when shares are issued at a price above their nominal value.

175 D

A statement of cash flows shows the inflows and outflows of cash for an entity not just for operating activities but also relating to investing activities and financing activities.

176 C

Revenue reserves are the retained earnings of an entity and would be increased only with option C. A would increase capital reserves, B would decrease revenue reserves and increase general reserves and D would increase the assets.

177 $289,100

Purchases can be found by constructing a control account:

	$		$
Cash paid	271,150	Opening payables	71,300
Discount received	6,600	**Purchases ($360,400 – $71,300)**	**289,100**
Goods returned	13,750		
Closing payables	68,900		
	360,400		360,400

178 $237,000

Sales can be found by constructing a sales control account:

	$		$
Receivables at 1.1.03	30,000	Receipts less cash sales	240,000
Sales ($267,000 – $30,000)	237,000	Receivables at 31.12.03	27,000
	267,000		267,000

179 A

The cost of goods withdrawn from the business by the owner is credited against the cost of purchases to ensure that purchases consist only of goods purchased for resale.

180 D

Transfers between revenue reserves, as mentioned in A and B, have no effect on the overall total of revenue reserves; issuing shares at a premium increases capital reserves; the paying of dividends must be from revenue reserves, so these will decrease.

ANALYSIS OF FINANCIAL STATEMENTS

IDENTIFY INFORMATION PROVIDED BY ACCOUNTING RATIOS

181 If an entity revalues its land and buildings the value of the capital employed will **increase**.

If an entity has property, plant and equipment which are coming to the end of their expected useful lives, this will result in an **increase** to ROCE.

If an entity invests in new property, plant and equipment, this will **decrease** ROCE in the short term.

182

Sales revenue over the years has remained stable, but costs have increased.	decrease
Sales revenue and costs have both decreased but costs by a greater proportion.	increase
There was a change in the sales mix which resulted in a higher proportion of more profitable products being sold in the current year.	increase
The business won new trade discounts with key suppliers.	increase

183

Operating a JIT inventory system.	decrease
Stock-piling inventory in preparation for a new sales drive.	increase
Increasing sales in the year.	no impact
Negotiating new contracts with suppliers which include increased discounts.	no impact

CALCULATE BASIC ACCOUNTING RATIOS

184 $500

		$	
Selling price (SP)	140	700	
Cost of sales (COS)	100	500	700 × 100/140
Gross profit	40	???	

185 7.5 times

Rate of inventories turnover is found by dividing cost of goods sold by average inventory. Average inventory is:

$$\left[\frac{24{,}000 + 20{,}000}{2}\right] = \$22{,}000$$

$$\text{Inventory turnover} = \frac{\text{Cost of sales}}{\text{Average inventory}}$$

	$
Opening inventory	24,000
Purchases	160,000
	184,000
Less: Closing inventory	(20,000)
Cost of goods sold	164,000

Rate of inventory turnover is therefore 164,000/22,000 = 7.5 times

186 D

You need only know the correct formula here.

187 A

The gearing ratio is the proportion of long-term loans to shareholders' funds, thus it follows that if a decrease in long-term loans is less than a decrease in the shareholders' funds, the gearing ratio will rise.

188 The current ratio is current assets: current liabilities, that is 5,800:2,200 = 2.6:1.

The quick ratio is current assets minus inventory: current liabilities, that is 2,000:2,200 = 0.9:1.

189 D

	$
Opening inventories	9,075
Add: Purchases	36,325
	45,400
Less: Closing inventories	(4,500)
Cost of sales (i.e. 70% of sales revenue)	40,900

	%	
Sales revenue	100	
Cost of sales	70	
Gross profit	30	$17,529 (i.e. 30/70 × $40,900)

190 49 Days

44,000/324,500 × 365 days = 49 days

Average inventories/COS × 365

Average inventories = (50,000 + 38,000)/2 = 44,000

191 51 Days

60,000/430,000 × 365 days = 51 days

Trade receivables/Sales × 365

192 47 Days

40,000/312,500 × 365 days = 47 days

Trade payables/Purchases × 365

193 1.93:1

108,000/56,000 = 1.93:1

Current assets: Current liabilities

Current assets = Trade receivables 60,000 + Prepayments 4,000 + Cash in hand 6,000 + Closing inventories 38,000 = 108,000

Current liabilities = Bank overdraft 8,000 + Trade payables 40,000 + Accruals 3,000 + Declared dividends 5,000 = 56,000

194 1.25:1

(108,000 – 38,000)/56,000 = 1.25:1

(Current assets – Inventories) : Current liabilities

Current assets and liabilities as above

195 53 Days

Cash cycle = Inventories days + Receivables days – Payables days = 49 + 51 – 47 (as per answers above) = 53 days

196 $80,000

$32,000/0.4 = $80,000

Current ratio is 1.4:1 and

Current assets – Current liabilities = 32,000

If Current liabilities are A then Current assets are 1.4A

1.4A – A = 32,000; 0.4A = 32,000

Hence A = 32,000/0.4 = Current liabilities

197 $40,000

Current liabilities = $80,000; Current assets = $80,000 × 1.4 = $112,000

Quick assets = $80,000 × 0.9 = $72,000

Therefore, inventories will be the difference between current assets and quick assets ($112,000 – 72,000) = $40,000

198 $468,000

Cost of sales = $40,000 × 8.775 = $351,000; Gross profit is 25% of sales

Therefore, sales equals to $351,000/0.75 = $468,000

199 $18,000

Closing receivables = $468,000 × 6/52 = $54,000

Current assets = $112,000 (see answer 180)

Closing inventories = $40,000 (see answer 180)

Bank balance = $112,000 – $54,000 – $40,000 = $18,000

200 A

Capital employed is increased by making a profit, or by adding more capital. Writing off irrecoverable debt would reduce profit; transactions such as C and D merely adjust the split of assets and liabilities but do not add anything overall.

Section 3

PRACTICE ASSESSMENT QUESTIONS

1 Which one of the following items should be classified as capital expenditure?

A Repairs to motor vans

B Depreciation of machinery

C Extension of premises

D Purchase of motor vans for resale

2 Match the following users with their principal information requirements:

	Users		Requirements
1	The public	A	The ability of the company to continue, and to pay pensions in the future
2	The government	B	The use of information for taking operational decisions in running the company
3	Employees	C	The policies of a company and how those policies affect the community, for example health and safety
4	Internal users	D	The performance and financial position of a company and its ability to pay dividends
5	Shareholders	E	The ability of a company to pay taxes, and administer other taxes, for example value-added tax

3 The form and content of management accounts used by an entity are specified by

A company law

B company law and international accounting standards

C the shareholders

D directors

4 The accounting convention that, in times of rising prices, tends to understate asset values and overstate profits, is the

A going concern convention

B prudence convention

C realisation convention

D historical cost convention

5 Using the available drag and drop options below complete the following statement.

Recording the purchase of computer stationery by debiting the computer equipment account would result in _________ of profit and __________ of non-current assets.

Available options:

an overstatement/an understatement/no change

(each option can be used more than once)

6 What does 'Limited' mean in an entity's name e.g.' ABC Limited'?

A A company's liability is limited to the total amount of its authorised share capital

B A company's liability is limited to the total amount of its issued share capital

C The members' liability is limited to the total amount paid or payable on the shares held by them

D The members' liability is limited to the nominal value of the shares held by them

7 Drag and drop the correct option from the list provided to complete the following statement.

The core objective of accounting is ____________________________________.

Options available:

to provide financial information to the users of such information/to maintain records of assets and liabilities/to keep a record of transactions/to fulfil statutory requirements

8 Which three of the following items are qualitative characteristics of financial statements in accordance with the IASB's Conceptual Framework for Financial Reporting?

A Relevance

B Comparability

C Profitability

D Understandability

E Accountability

9 Sharon started a business on 1 January 20X1 with $30,000 capital. During the year 20X1 she withdrew $15,000 from the business and paid in a gift of $9,000 from her uncle. At 31 December 20X1 the business's net assets were valued at $54,000.

Calculate the business profit for the year.

$___________

10 An imprest system is designed to help reconcile the cash book with the bank statement.

Is this statement true or false?

True/False

11 The following information relates to PQR's receivables:

	$
Balance b/f at 1 January 20X3	166,200
Allowance for receivables at 1 January 20X3	13,320
Increase in provision during 20X3	1,440
Discount allowed in year	47,280
Sales in year	1,460,760
Contra purchase ledger in year	106,800
Receipts from customers in year	1,370,400

What was the balance carried forward at 31 December 20X3 on PQR's sales ledger control account?

$__________

12 JOB purchased goods on credit from SAD for $24,000.

Using the drop down lists provided in the table below identify the correct accounting entries to record this transaction.

Debit/Credit	**Account**
Debit	Purchases/Receivables/Payables/Cash/Sales
Credit	Purchases/Receivables/Payables/Cash/Sales

13 ALP owed $60 to trade payables at 1 July 20X4 and $90 at 30 June 20X5. Purchases on credit amounted to $3,000 during the year and suppliers allowed a total of $150 cash discount.

How much cash was paid to suppliers during the year?

$__________

14 Red operates the imprest system for petty cash. At 1 March there was a float of $200, but it was decided to increase this to $250 at the 31 March. During March, the petty cashier received $40 from a member of staff who had claimed excessive expenses in a previous month. The cashier then paid $75 for drinks and biscuits, $72 for stationery and $40 for window cleaning.

How much was withdrawn from the bank account for petty cash at the end of March?

$__________

15 Assuming that it reconciles with the cash book, how would a balance marked 'Cr' on a business's bank statement be classified in an entity's statement of financial position?

A Current asset

B Current liability

C Non-current asset

D Non-current liability

16 A purchases day book total $7,390 had been entered in the control account as $7,930.

What will be the impact when the required correction is made?

	Control account	List of balances
A	Debit $540	No effect
B	Debit $540	Decrease total by $540
C	Credit $540	No effect
D	Debit $1,080	No effect

17 At 31 December 20X4, an entity's cash book had a debit balance of $8,400. The bank statement at that date had an overdrawn balance of $2,520.

Which one of the following timing differences could account for the discrepancy?

A Cheques drawn but not yet presented amounted to $5,880

B Cheques received but not yet cleared amounted to $5,880

C Cheques drawn but not yet presented amounted to $10,920

D Cheques received but not yet cleared amounted to $10,920

18 Which of the following errors would not cause there to be a difference in the trial balance?

A incomplete double entry

B addition error

C transaction not recorded at all

D transposition error in the debit entry

19 State whether each of the following two statements are true or false

A An integrated report contains only historical financial information

True/False

B An integrated report is the same thing as the notes to the financial statements

True/False

20 GRE paid $3,600 insurance during the year to 31 March 20X1.

As at 1 April 20X0 GRE had overpaid $1,200, and the correct charge in the statement of profit or loss for year to 31 March 20X1 was $3,900.

What was the amount of the prepayment at 31 March 20X1?

$___________

21 **Drag and drop the correct option from the list provided to complete the following statement.**

Businesses charge depreciation on non-current assets in order to ____________________.

Options available:

ensure that sufficient funds are available to replace the assets/

spread the cost of the assets over their estimated useful life/

comply with the prudence convention/

reduce profits and dividends

22 An entity purchased a car for $60,000 on 1 July 20X3 and expected it to have a useful life of 5 years. It depreciated the car using 50% reducing balance and sold it on 30 June 20X6 for $30,000.

What was the profit on disposal?

$__________

23 GRA has the following balances in its trial balance at 31 December 20X3.

	$
Total receivables	420,000
Irrecoverable debts written off (no previous allowance)	3,000
Allowance for receivables at 1 January 20X3	30,000

GRA wishes to carry forward an allowance for receivables equal to 10% of total receivables.

What is the total effect of the above on the statement of profit or loss for the year ended 31 December 20X3?

A A charge of $14,700

B A credit of $14,700

C A charge of $15,000

D A credit of $15,000

24 **Under which heading should debentures be classified in an entity's statement of financial position?**

A Equity

B Current assets

C Current liabilities

D Non-current liabilities

25 KIR sells three products X, Y and Z. At KIR's reporting date the inventories held were as follows:

	Cost	Selling price
	$	$
X	3,600	4,500
Y	18,600	18,300
Z	2,760	2,790

At sale a 5% commission is payable by KIR to its agent.

What was the total value these inventories in KIR's financial statements?

A $23,636

B $24,282

C $24,960

D $25,635

26 DEF sold goods with a list price of $1,000 to Khan which was subject to trade discount of 5% and early settlement discount of 4% if the invoice was paid within 7 days. The normal credit period available to credit customers is 30 days from invoice date. At the point of sale, Khan was not expected to take advantage of early settlement terms offered. Khan subsequently paid within 7 days.

What accounting entries should be made by DEF to record settlement of the amount due?

A Debit Cash $950, Debit Revenue $50 and Credit Trade receivables $1,000

B Debit Cash $950, Credit Revenue $38 and Credit Trade receivables $912

C Debit Cash $912, Debit Revenue $38 and Credit Trade receivables $950

D Debit Cash $912, and Credit Trade receivables $912

27 An entity sold goods with a net value of $200,000 and made purchases with a gross value of $162,000. All transactions were subject to sales tax at the rate of 20%.

What was the balance on the sales tax account based upon this information?

A $933

B $6,333

C $7,600

D $13,000

28 HEO sold a motor van which it had purchased three years ago at a cost of $24,000 and which it depreciated each year at 50% using the reducing balance method.

HEO traded this van in for a new vehicle which had a cost of $36,000, and paid the supplying garage $34,400 by cheque.

Using the number entry field and the drop down text below – what was the profit or loss on the sale of the old van?

$____________ profit/loss

29 EUR owns property which it lets to tenants, MED and ORE. EUR is currently preparing its financial statements for the year ended 31 December 20X6. The following information is available:

	Medea	**Orestes**
	$	$
Rent paid in advance 31.12.X5	1,000	
Rent owed 31.12.X5		1,400
Rent paid during year	4,000	5,000
Rent paid in advance at 31.12.X6		500
Rent owed at 31.12.X6	200	

What figure for rental income will appear in EUR's statement of profit or loss for the year ended 31 December 20X6?

A $8,300

B $8,900

C $9,100

D $9,700

30 BOW's accounting year end is 31 December. For various reasons, inventories could not be counted as at 31 December 20X5 until 6 January 20X6. The inventories were counted on 6 January 20X6 and, at that date, were valued at $445,800. Detailed records were kept of inventories movements between the 31 December 20X5 and the physical inventory count on 6 January 20X6. The following figures (all stated at cost) are available:

	$
Sales	7,500
Purchases	6,930
Returns inwards	1,650
Returns outwards	840

In accordance with IAS 2 *Inventories*, what was BOW's inventory valuation at 31 December 20X5?

$____________

31 **MRM paid rent of $14,400 for the period 1 January 20X4 to 31 December 20X4. MRM's financial statements prepared for the nine months ended 30 September 20X4 should include which of the following amounts?**

A Only a rent expense of $10,800

B A rent expense of $10,800 and a prepayment of $3,600

C A rent expense of $10,800 and accrued revenue of $3,600

D A rent expense of $14,400 with an explanatory note that this is the charge for twelve months

32 ATO purchased a machine for which the supplier's list price was $162,000. ATO paid $117,000 cash and traded in an old machine which had a carrying amount of $72,000. It is ATO's policy to depreciate such machines at the rate of 10% per annum on cost.

What was the carrying amount of the machine after one year?

A $105,300

B $145,800

C $170,100

D $172,800

33 **Using the drag and drop options available below complete the following statement.**

The difference between a statement of profit or loss and an income and expenditure statement is that____________________________________.

Options available:

an income and expenditure statement is an alternative international accounting term for a statement of profit or loss

a statement of profit or loss prepared for a business entity and an income and expenditure statement is prepared for a non-profit-making organisation

a statement of profit or loss is prepared on an accruals basis and an income and expenditure account is prepared on a cash flow basis

a statement of profit or loss is prepared for a manufacturing business and an income and expenditure statement is prepared for a non-manufacturing business

34 The following information is given for DEF for the year ended 31 October 20X0:

	$
Purchase of raw materials	28,000
Returns inwards	2,000
Increase in inventories of raw materials	850
Direct wages	10,500
Carriage inwards	1,250
Production overheads	7,000
Decrease in work-in-progress	2,500

What was the DEF's factory cost of goods completed?

$____________

35 **Which one of the following costs should be included in the calculation of prime cost in a manufacturing account?**

A Cost of transporting raw materials from suppliers premises

B Wages of factory workers engaged in machine maintenance

C Depreciation of lorries used for deliveries to customers

D Cost of indirect production materials

36 FRE's inventories on 1 January 20X4 cost $14,300 and its payables were $3,750. During the year, sales amounted to $174,000, earning an average mark-up of 33% on cost. FRE paid $133,650 to suppliers during the year and payables' balances at 31 December 20X4 totalled $4,900. On the same date FRE's shop was burgled and all inventories were stolen.

What was the cost of the stolen inventories?

A $16,300

B $18,273

C $30,800

D $33,100

37 **The reducing-balance method of depreciating non-current assets is more appropriate than the straight-line method when:**

A there is no expected residual value for the asset

B the expected life of the asset is not capable of being estimated

C the asset is expected to be replaced in a short period of time

D it more accurately reflects the consumption of the asset

38 **Which of the following items should be classified as revenue expenditure?**

A Drawings of goods for private consumption by the proprietor

B Petrol for proprietor's wife's private car

C Purchase of a new word processor

D Purchase of an ink cartridge for the word processor

39 A business entity had opening inventories of $24,000 and closing inventories of $36,000. During the accounting period, it made purchase returns of $10,000. The cost of goods sold was $222,000.

What was the cost of purchases?

$____________

40 At 30 June 20X7, TRE had issued share capital of $10,000, consisting of ordinary shares of $0.50 each, a share premium account of $5,000 and retained earnings of $57,000. TRE made a bonus issue of shares of 'one for five' on 30 June 20X7.

Select from the items available to state the accounting entries required to record this issue of shares along with the value of the transaction.

		$
Debit	Cash/Share capital/Share premium	$1,000/$2,000/$4,000
Credit	Cash/Share capital/Share premium	$1,000/$2,000/$4,000

41 Classify each of the following costs as either an expense or an intangible asset that should be capitalised in accordance with IAS 38 *Intangible Assets*.

	Expense	**Intangible asset**
Employee training costs		
Plant and machinery running costs		
Cost of purchasing a five-year product licence		
Market research costs		

42 CLA paid $20,400 cash for electricity during the year ended 31 December 20X3. At 1 January 20X3 CLA owed $15,000 and at 31 December 20X3 it owed $17,400.

What charge for electricity should appear in CLA's statement of profit or loss for the year ended 31 December 20X3?

A $17,400

B $18,000

C $20,400

D $22,800

43 What action does an entity need to take upon discovery that a major customer has become insolvent? An allowance for this receivable had been made at the end of the previous year.

The entries required to write off the amount outstanding are:

A	Dr Irrecoverable debts	Cr Receivables
B	Dr Receivables	Cr Irrecoverable debts
C	Dr Receivables	Cr Allowance for receivables
D	Dr Allowance for receivables	Cr Receivables

44 Which one of the following statements best defines an expense?

A An expense is an outflow of economic benefits resulting from a claim by a third party

B An expense is a decrease in assets or increase in liabilities that result in a decreases in equity, other than those relating to distributions to holders of equity claims

C An expense is any outflow of economic benefits in an accounting period

D An expense is an outflow of economic benefits resulting from the purchase of resources in an accounting period

45 In which financial statements would you expect to include a loss on disposal of property plant and equipment? Choose all that apply.

A The statement of cash flows

B The statement of financial position

C The statement of profit or loss and other comprehensive income

D The statement of changes in equity

46 XYZ's plant and machinery had a carrying value of $450,000 at the year end. Its opening balance was $325,000. During the year, depreciation of $63,000 was charged and an asset with a carrying value of $12,000 was disposed of resulting in a profit on disposal of $3,000.

What it the cash outflow for purchases of plant and machinery in the year?

$____________

47 CAN returned some goods to a supplier because they were faulty. The original purchase price of these goods was $24,780.

The ledger clerk treated the return correctly on both the payables' ledger control account and the individual payables' account, but debited the purchase returns account with $25,860.

Using the drop downs available in the table below to show the correcting entry that needs to be made.

Debit/Credit	**Account**	**Amount**
Debit	Purchases returns/Receivables returns/ Suspense/Cash/Payables	$1080/$50,640
Credit	Purchases returns/Receivables returns/ Suspense/Cash/Payables	$1080/$50,640

48 **An entity had the following trading account for the year ending 31 May 2008:**

	$	$
Sales revenue		90,000
Opening inventory	8,000	
Add: Purchases	53,000	
	———	
	61,000	
Less: Closing inventory	(12,000)	
	———	(49,000)
		———
Gross profit		41,000
		———

What was its rate of inventory turnover for the year?

____________ times (to 1 decimal place)

49 The financial statements of FGH for the years ended 30 September 20X3 and 20X4 respectively included the following:

	20X3	**20X4**
	$	$
Share capital of $1 each	40,000	46,000
Share premium	10,000	12,000
Retained earnings	63,000	72,500

During the year ended 30 September 20X4, loan notes of $8,000 at par were issued.

What was the net cash inflow or outflow from financing activities during the year ended 30 September 20X4?

____________ Inflow/outflow (delete which does not apply)

50 KLN recorded the following transactions in its financial statements for the year ended 31 October 20X6:

- a revaluation surplus of $15,000 on revaluation of property
- depreciation charge of $4,200
- loss on disposal of property, plant and equipment of $3250

What amount should be included in 'other comprehensive income' within the statement of profit or loss and other comprehensive income for the year ended 31 October 20X6?

$____________

51 WXY provided the following information relating to its financial statements for the year ended 28 February 20X5:

	$	$
Sales revenue		372,640
Less: Cost of goods sold		
Inventories at 1 March 20X4	13,750	
Purchases	298,957	
Less: inventory at 28 February 20X5	???	
	______	
		______
Gross profit		???
		______

Subsequently, WXY identified that the sales revenue figure should have been stated as $372,463 and that sales returns of $2,468 and purchases returns of $4,268 had been omitted form the information above. WXY earns a 20% gross profit margin on sales.

What was WXY's value of inventories at 28 February 20X5?

$____________

52 An entity's cash book had an opening balance in the bank column of $900 credit. 'The following transactions then took place:

- cash sales $2,300 including sales tax of $300
- receipts from customers of $7,200
- payments to payables of $5,000 less 5% cash discount
- dishonoured cheques from customers amounting to $400.

The closing balance in the bank column of the cash book should be:

$____________ debit/credit.

53 Following extraction of a trial balance, INT created a suspense account with a debit balance of $2,250. Upon investigation, the following errors were found:

- the closing balance of the purchase ledger control account had been overcast by $2,100
- the purchase returns daybook had been overcast by $660.
- The list of purchase ledger balances included a debit balance of $400 which had been counted as a credit balance when arriving at the total of the purchase ledger balances

When these items had been corrected, what was the balance remaining on the suspense account?

$____________ debit/credit.

54 **An entity made a profit of $4,000 but its bank balance has fallen by $2,500. This could be due to**

A depreciation of $1,500 and an increase in inventories of $5,000

B depreciation of $3,000 and the repayment of a loan of $3,500

C depreciation of $6,000 and the purchase of new non-current assets for $12,500

D the disposal of a non-current asset for $6,500 less than its carrying amount

55 JAD received cash from JOS in part-payment of an amount owed.

Using the drop down menus available in the table below select the correct accounting entries to record the receipt of cash by JAD.

Debit	Credit
Cash/Sales/Payables/Receivables	**Cash/Sales/Payables/Receivables**

56 **Which THREE of the following statements relating to depreciation are true?**

A Accounting for depreciation reduces the profit for the year

B Accounting for depreciation generates cash for the business

C Not all items of property, plant and equipment are depreciated

D Accounting for depreciation does not result in a cash outflow

E The same method and rate of depreciation should be applied to all items of property, plant and equipment

57 PQR sold goods with a list price of $4,500 to Singh which was subject to trade discount of 5% and early settlement discount of 4% if the invoice was paid within 7 days. The normal credit period available to credit customers is 30 days from invoice date. At the point of sale, Singh was expected to take advantage of the early settlement terms offered. However, on this occasion, Singh did not pay within 7 days.

What accounting entries should be made by PQR to record settlement of the amount outstanding?

A Debit Cash $4,104, Debit Revenue $396 and Credit Trade receivables $4,500

B Debit Cash $4,275, Debit Discount received $171 and Credit Trade receivables $4,104

C Debit Cash $4,275 and Credit Trade receivables $4,275

D Debit Cash $4,275, Credit Trade receivables $4,104 and Credit Revenue $171

58 **Using the drag and drop options available, complete the following statement.**

Goodwill is most appropriately classed as ____________________.

Available options:

a current asset/an intangible asset/a fictitious liability/a semi-non-current asset

59 **Which one of the following is most likely to increase the trade receivables collection period?**

A Offering credit customers a significant discount for prompt payment within seven days of receipt of the invoice

B Paying suppliers promptly within seven days of receipt of invoice

C An increased volume of credit sales in comparison with the previous accounting period

D Poor application of credit control by an entity

60 JKL had tangible non-current assets with a carrying amount of $60,000 at 31 May 20X8 and $57,600 at 31 May 20X9. During the year ended 31 May 2019, JKL charged depreciation of $8,500 and disposed of property plant and equipment which had cost $6,000 and on which accumulated depreciation was $2,500.

What was the cash paid for property, plant and equipment additions during the year ended 31 May 20X9?

$__________

Section 4

ANSWERS TO PRACTICE ASSESSMENT QUESTIONS

1 **C**

2 **1C, 2E, 3A, 4B, 5D**

3 **D**

4 **D**

5 Recording the purchase of computer stationery by debiting the computer equipment account would result in an **overstatement** of profit and an **overstatement** of non-current assets.

6 **C**

7 The core objective of accounting is **to provide financial information to the users of such information**.

8 **A, B and D**

9 **$30,000**

Initial capital – drawings + further capital introduced (legacy) +/– profit/(loss) = Closing capital (net assets)

30,000 – 15,000 + 9,000 +/– profit/(loss) = 54,000

Therefore profit = 54,000 – 30,000 + 15,000 – 9,000 = 30,000

10 **False**

The imprest system helps to control petty cash, not the bank account.

11 $102,480

SLCA

Bal b/f	166,200	Revenue (Discount allowed)	47,280
Sales	1,460,760	Contra purchase ledger	106,800
		Receipts from receivables	1,370,400
		Bal c/f (bal fig)	102,480
	1,626,960		1,626,960

12

Debit/Credit	Account
Debit	Purchases
Credit	Payables

13 $2,820

Payables

	$		$
Discount received	150	Bal b/d	60
Cash (bal. fig.)	2,820	Purchases	3,000
Bal c/d	90		
	3,060		3,060

14 $197

	$
Opening petty cash float	200
Received from member of staff	40
Paid out in expenses (75 + 72 + 40)	(187)
	53
From bank account (bal fig)	197
Required closing cash float	250

15 A

16 A

17 **D**

Cheques received were lodged into the bank but were not yet cleared.

18 **C**

19 **Both statements are FALSE**

20 **$900**

Insurance

	$		$
Bal b/d	1,200	Statement of profit or loss	3,900
Cash	3,600	Bal c/d	900
	4,800		4,800

21 Businesses charge depreciation on non-current assets in order to **spread the cost of the assets over their estimated useful life**.

22 **$22,500**

	$
Cost	60,000
Depreciation year 1: $60,000 × 50%	(30,000)
	30,000
Depreciation year 2: $30,000 × 50%	(15,000)
	15,000
Depreciation year 3: $7,500 × 50%	(7,500)
	7,500

Non-current asset disposal account

	$		$
Cost (original cost always)	60,000	Accumulated depreciation	52,500
SP&L (balancing figure)	22,500	Sale proceeds	30,000
	82,500		82,500

23 C

Allowance for receivables

	$		$
Bal c/d (10% × 420,000)	42,000	Bal b/d	30,000
		Irrec. debts a/c	12,000
	42,000		42,000

Irrecoverable debts expense

	$		$
Allowance for receivables	12,000	Statement of profit or loss	15,000
Irrec. debts written off	3,000		
	15,000		15,000

Note: Since the irrecoverable debt write off appears in the trial balance, receivables must already have been adjusted.

24 D

A debenture is a long-term loan. It should be classified as a non-current liability.

25 A

In accordance with IAS 2 *Inventories*, inventories are valued at lower of cost and net realisable value (costs to be incurred in selling inventories are deducted from selling price in computing NRV).

	Cost	**Price less commission**	**Lower of cost and NRV**
A	3,600	4,275	3,600
B	18,600	17,385	17,385
C	2,760	2,651	2,651
			23,636

Here each item A, B and C are considered separately and not collectively as a group.

26 C

Trade discount is always deducted when calculating the amount invoiced by the seller. In addition, as Khan was not expected to take account of the early settlement discount terms, the amount of revenue receivable is calculated after deduction of trade discount only at $950 ($1000 × 95%).

When Khan subsequently pays early to be eligible for the discount, the accounting entries should reflect that fact and record settlement of the amount outstanding and also reduced revenue.

Debit Cash $912 ($950 × 96%), Debit Revenue $38 ($950 × 4%), and Credit Trade receivables $950.

27 D

	$
Output sales tax on sales (20% × $200,000)	40,000
Input sales tax on purchases (20/120 × $162,000)	(27,000)
	13,000

28 $1,400 loss

Non-current asset disposal account

Cost	24,000	Accumulated depreciation	
Paid	34,400	New van	36,000
		SP&L	1,400
	58,400		58,400

12,000 + 6,000 + 3,000 = 21,000

Cost	24,000
Depreciation 50%	(12,000)
	12,000
Depreciation 50%	(6,000)
	6,000
Depreciation 50%	(3,000)

29 A

Rent receivable account

	$		$
Bal b/d (Orsetes)	1,400	Bal b/d (Medea)	1,000
SP&L (balancing figure)	8,300	Recorded in year (4,000 + 5,000)	9,000
Bal c/d (Orestes)	500	Bal c/d (Medea)	200
	10,200		10,200
Bal b/d (Medea)	200	Bal b/d (Orestes)	500

30 $445,560

445,800 + 7,500 – 6,930 – 1,650 + 840 = $445,560

31 B

14,400 × 9/12 = $10,800 Rent expense and 14,400 – 10,800 = $3,600 Prepayment

32 B

$162,000 × 90% = $145,800

The carrying amount of $72,000 of the trade-in old machine is irrelevant. The trade-in value agreed is evidently $45,000, which is the difference between the supplier's price and the cash paid.

33 The difference between a statement of profit or loss and an income and expenditure statement is that **a statement of profit or loss prepared for a business entity and an income and expenditure statement is prepared for a non-profit-making organisation**.

34 $48,400

	$
Purchase of raw material	28,000
Carriage inwards	1,250
Increase in inventories	(850)
Cost of material consumed	28,400
Direct wages	10,500
Prime cost	38,900
Production overheads	7,000
Decrease in work-in-progress	2,500
Production cost	48,400

35 A

The cost of transporting raw materials forms part of the direct material costs.

36 B

	$	
Sales	174,000	
Opening inventories	14,300	
Purchases (see below)	134,800	
	149,100	
Less: Closing inventories	$18,273	= Balancing figure
Cost of sales (see below)	130,827	

PLCA

	$		$
Paid payables	133,650	Bal b/f	3,750
Bal c/d	4,900	Purchases (balancing figure)	134,800
	138,550		138,550

	%		$
Balance	133%	Sales	174,000
Mark-up	100%	(Cost of sales)	???
Given	33%	Gross profit	

Therefore, cost of sales = $174,000 × 100/133 = $130,827

37 D

38 D

39 $244,000

Reconstruction of cost of goods sold to establish the purchases figure:

	$	$
Opening inventories		24,000
Add: Purchases	244,000*	
Less: Returns	(10,000)	234,000
Closing inventories		(36,000)
Cost of goods sold		222,000

*Found by difference

40

		$
Debit	Share premium	2,000
Credit	Share capital	2,000

Shares issued = $10,000 × 2 = 20,000 shares in issue /5 = 4,000 bonus shares at $0.5 each

41

	Expense	**Intangible asset**
Employee training costs	Yes	No
Plant and machinery running costs	Yes	No
Cost of purchasing a five-year product licence	No	Yes
Market research costs	Yes	No

42 D

Electricity

	$		$
Cash paid	20,400	Bal b/f	15,000
Bal c/d	17,400	SP&L	22,800
	37,800		37,800

43 A

D is wrong because the allowance for receivables is only adjusted at the end of each accounting period.

44 B

All other suggested answers include only part of the definition of an expense – they are not precise enough or comprehensive enough.

45 A and C

A loss on disposal of plant and equipment will be included in the statement of cash flows as an adjustment to profit before tax in arriving at net cash flows from operating activities and it will also be included in the statement of profit or loss and other comprehensive income.

46 $200,000

Plant and machinery

	$000		$000
Bal b/f	325	Depreciation	63
		Disposal	12
Additions	200	Bal c/f	450
(bal fig = cash paid)			
	525		525

47

Debit/Credit	**Account**	**Amount**
Debit	Suspense	$50,640
Credit	Purchases returns	$50,640

Correct entry was to credit purchases returns account with $24,780. To correct, credit purchases returns with $24,780 + $25,860. Suspense account is to be debited, as the original entry will have created a suspense account balance by putting the accounts out of balance.

48 4.9 times

Rate of inventory turnover is found by dividing cost of goods sold by average inventory.

Average inventory = (8,000 + 12,000)/2 = $10,000

Cost of goods sold is $49,000

Rate of inventory turnover is therefore 49,000/10,000 = 4.9 times

49 $16,000 inflow

	20X3	**20X4**
	$	$
Proceeds of share issue	($6,000 + $2,000)	8,000
Issue of loan notes		8,000
		16,000

50 $15,000

Only the revaluation surplus is included on 'other comprehensive income'. All other items are accounted for in the statement of profit or loss.

51 $12,443

	$	$
Sales revenue ($372,463 – $2,468)		369,995
Less: Cost of goods sold		
Inventories at 1 March 20X4	13,750	
Purchases ($298,957 – $4,268)	294,689	
Less: inventory at 28 February 20X5	(12,443)	
(80% × $369,995)		295,996
Gross profit (20% × $369,995)		73,999

52 $3,450 debit

The calculation is as follows:

	$
Opening overdraft	(900)
Add cash sales, including sales tax	2,300
Add receipts from customers	7,200
Less payments after discount	(4,750)
Less dishonoured cheques	(400)
Closing balance	3,450

53 $150 debit

Suspense account

	$		$
Balance per Trial Balance	2,250	Overstated PLCA balance	2,100
		Balance c/d	150
	2,250		2,250
Balance b/d	150		

The casting error in the purchase returns daybook affects debit balances and credit balances equally, so will not contribute towards clearing the suspense account balance. The list of purchase ledger balances is not part of the double entry accounting system and therefore will not contribute towards clearing the suspense account balance. The only error that contributes towards clearance of the suspense account is the casting error on the purchase ledger control account.

This is corrected by the following adjustment:

Debit: PLCA (to reduce the balance on the PLCA to the correct amount) $2,100

Credit: Suspense $2,100

54 C

	$
Profit	4,000
Add back depreciation	6,000
Net cash inflow	10,000
Purchase of non-current assets	(12,500)
Decrease	(2,500)

55

Debit	Credit
Cash	**Receivables**

56 A, C and D

57 D

Trade discount is always deducted when calculating the amount invoiced by the seller. In addition, as Khan is expected to take account of the early settlement discount terms, the amount of revenue receivable is calculated after deduction of both trade discount and early settlement discount, a total of $4,104 ($4,500 × 95% × 96%). When Khan subsequently pays outside the settlement discount period, the full amount of the receivable $4,275 ($4,500 × 95%) is due. The additional cash received in excess of the receivable amount of $171 is therefore accounted for as a cash sale as follows:

Debit Cash $4,275, Credit Trade receivables $4,104 and Credit Revenue $171.

58 Goodwill is most appropriately classed **as an intangible asset as per IAS 38 *Intangible Assets***.

Goodwill arises when more is paid for the net assets of a business than their fair value. Thus, an additional asset is acquired; it is intangible and should be subject to regular impairment reviews to check that the goodwill is not overstated in the statement of financial position.

59 D

If a significant discount is offered to credit customers, some will be likely to take advantage of this, and therefore reduce the trade receivables collection period. Any decisions relating to payment of trade payables will not affect the trade receivables collection period. An increase in the volume of credit sales will not, in itself, increase the trade receivables collection period.

60 $9,600

Property, plant and equipment

	$		$
Bal b/f	60,000	Depreciation	8,500
		Disposal ($6,000-$2,500)	3,500
Cash paid	9,600	Bal c/f	57,600
	69,600		69,600

Section 5

REFERENCES

The Board (2024) IAS 1 *Presentation of Financial Statements.* London: IFRS Foundation

The Board (2024) IAS 2 *Inventories*. London: IFRS Foundation.

The Board (2024) IAS 7 *Statement of Cash Flows.* London: IFRS Foundation

The Board (2024) IAS 16 *Property, Plant and Equipment*. London: IFRS Foundation.

The Board (2024) IAS 38 *Intangible Assets*. London: IFRS Foundation.

The Board (2024) *The Conceptual Framework for Financial Reporting*. London: IFRS Foundation